Doodle
Synthesis

An Intense Coloring Book Made for everyone

Illustrations by: Rocky Villaruel

Cover Colored and Designed by: Regina Lanuza

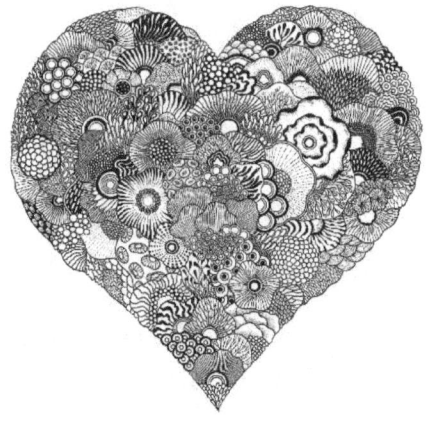

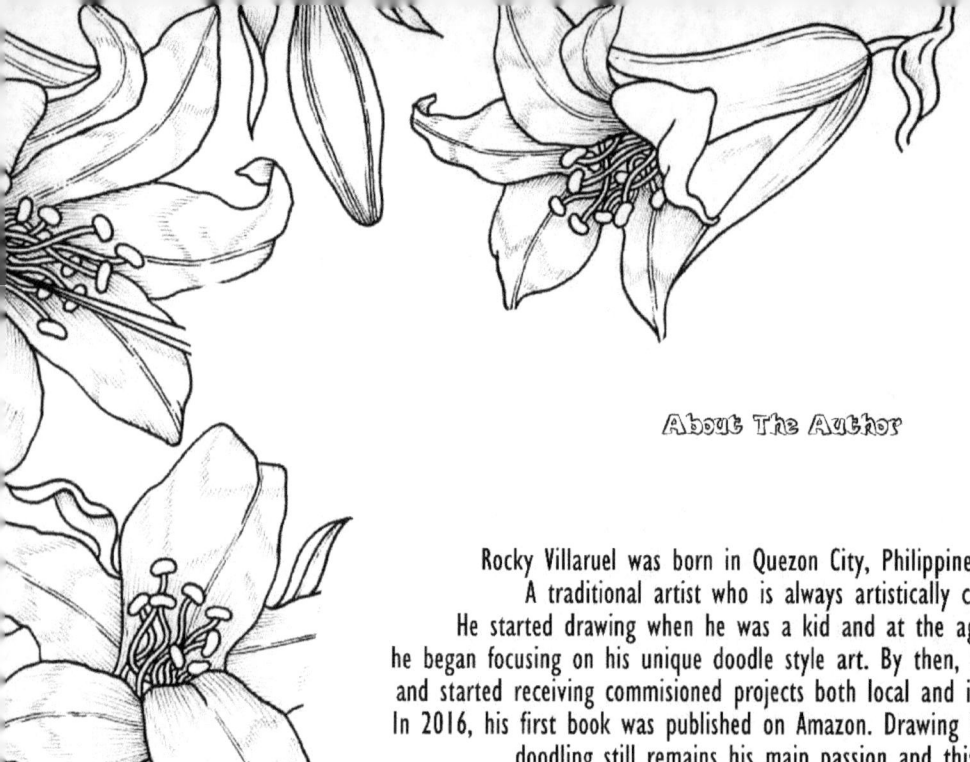
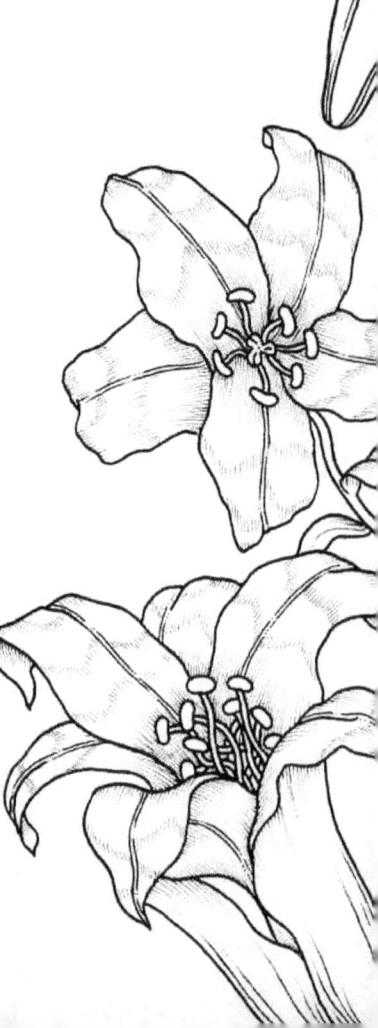

About The Author

Rocky Villaruel was born in Quezon City, Philippines in 1995.
A traditional artist who is always artistically creative.
He started drawing when he was a kid and at the age of fourteen,
he began focusing on his unique doodle style art. By then, his work was noticed
and started receiving commisioned projects both local and international clients.
In 2016, his first book was published on Amazon. Drawing intricate line art and
doodling still remains his main passion and this year he
decided to quit his day job to pursue a career as a freelance illustrator.

For more information about Rocky Villaruel's work visit
www.rockyvillaruel.com
Or follow his social media accounts
Twitter: @rockyvillaruel
Instagram: @rockyvillaruel
Facebook: All about Doodle by Rocky Villaruel
Behance: Rocky Villaruel

Copyright ©2018 www.rockyvillaruel.com
Doodle Synthesis
ISBN-13: 978-1720538882
ISBN-10: 1720538883
All rights reserved.
No part of this book may be reproduced or transmitted in any form or by any means,
electronic, mechanical, including photocopying, recording, or by any information storage and
retrieval system without the written permission of the author, except permitted by law.

Author: Rocky Villaruel
Editor: Jenkie Fontanilla
Cover Design: Regina Lanuza

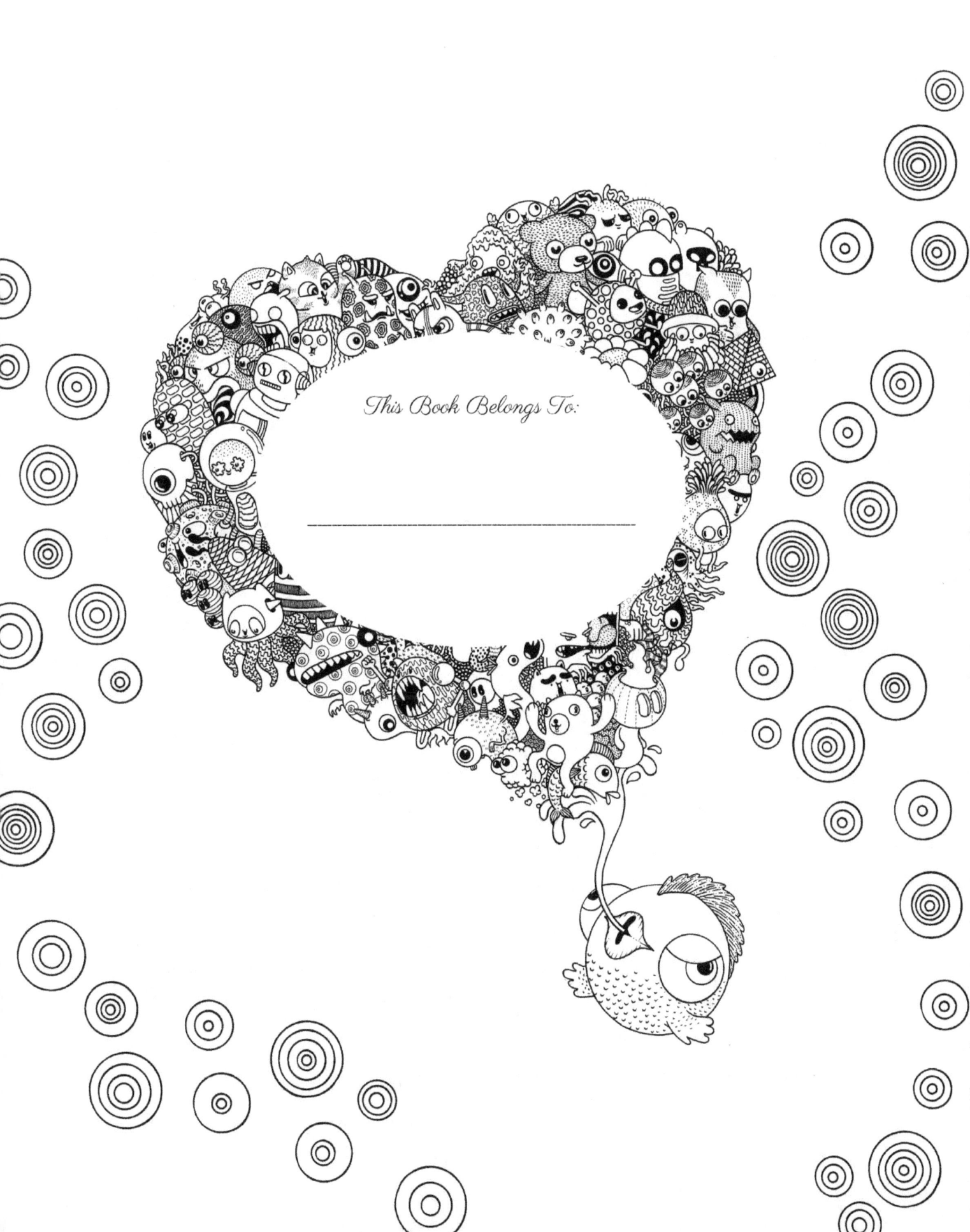

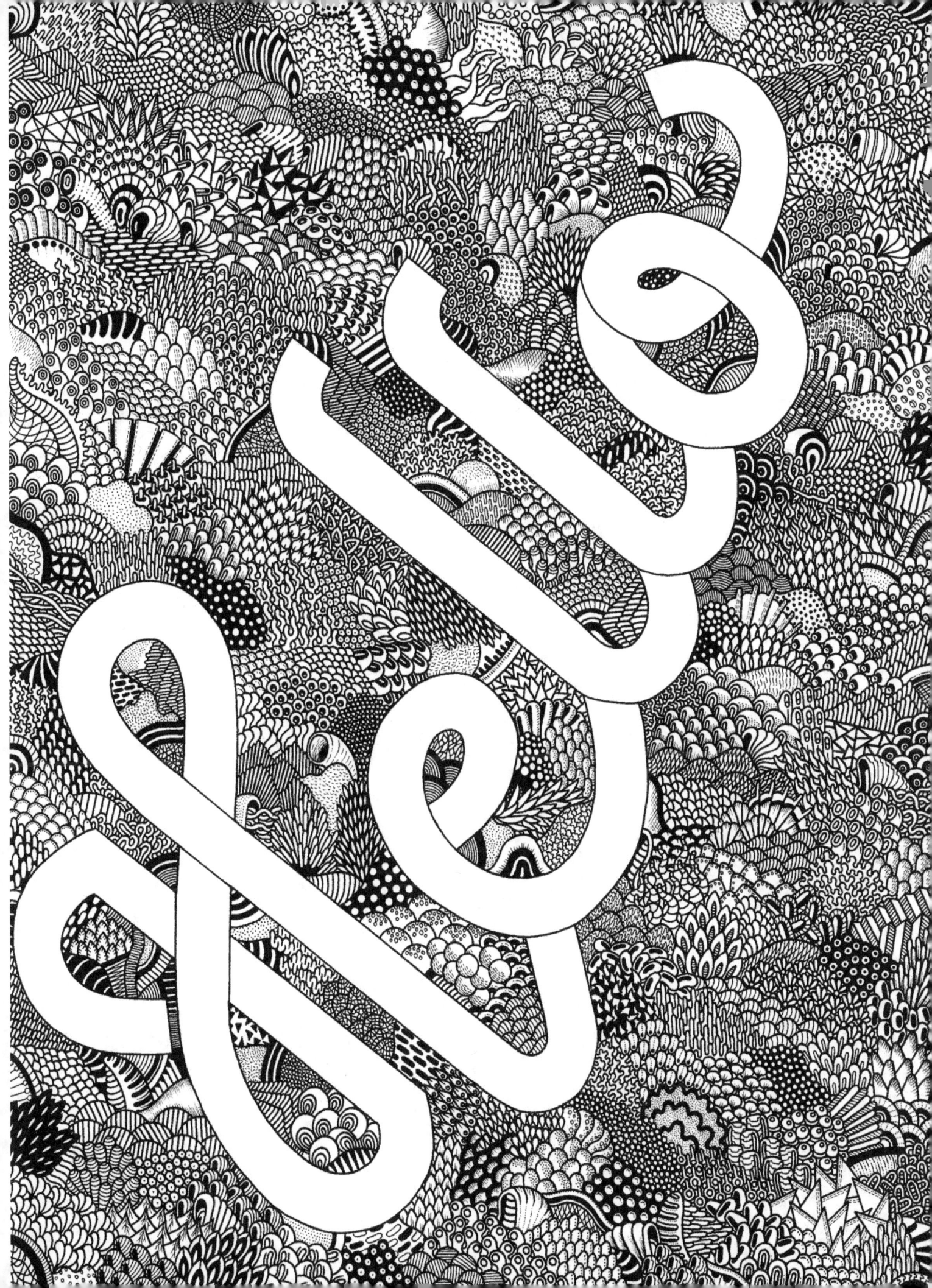

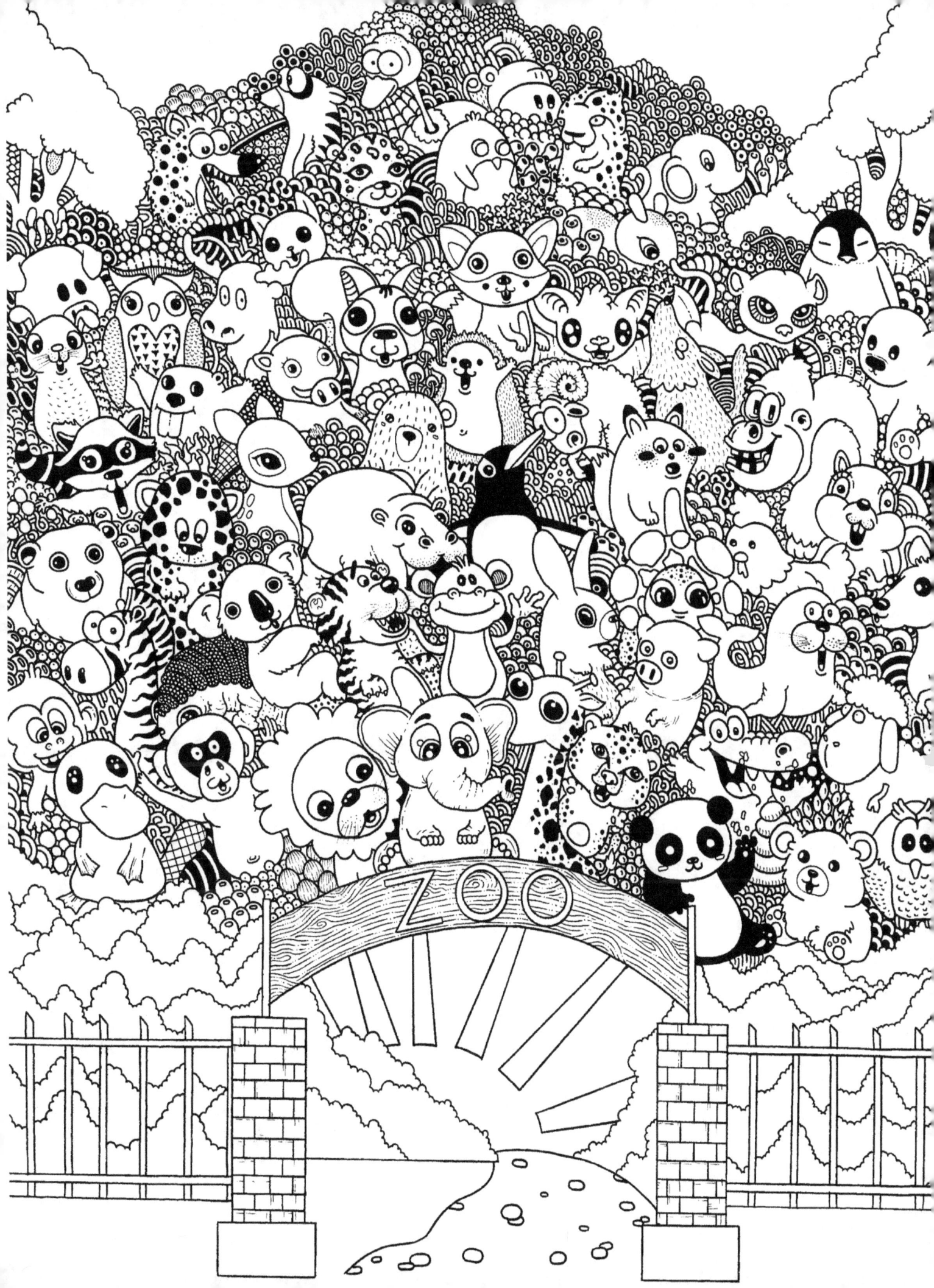

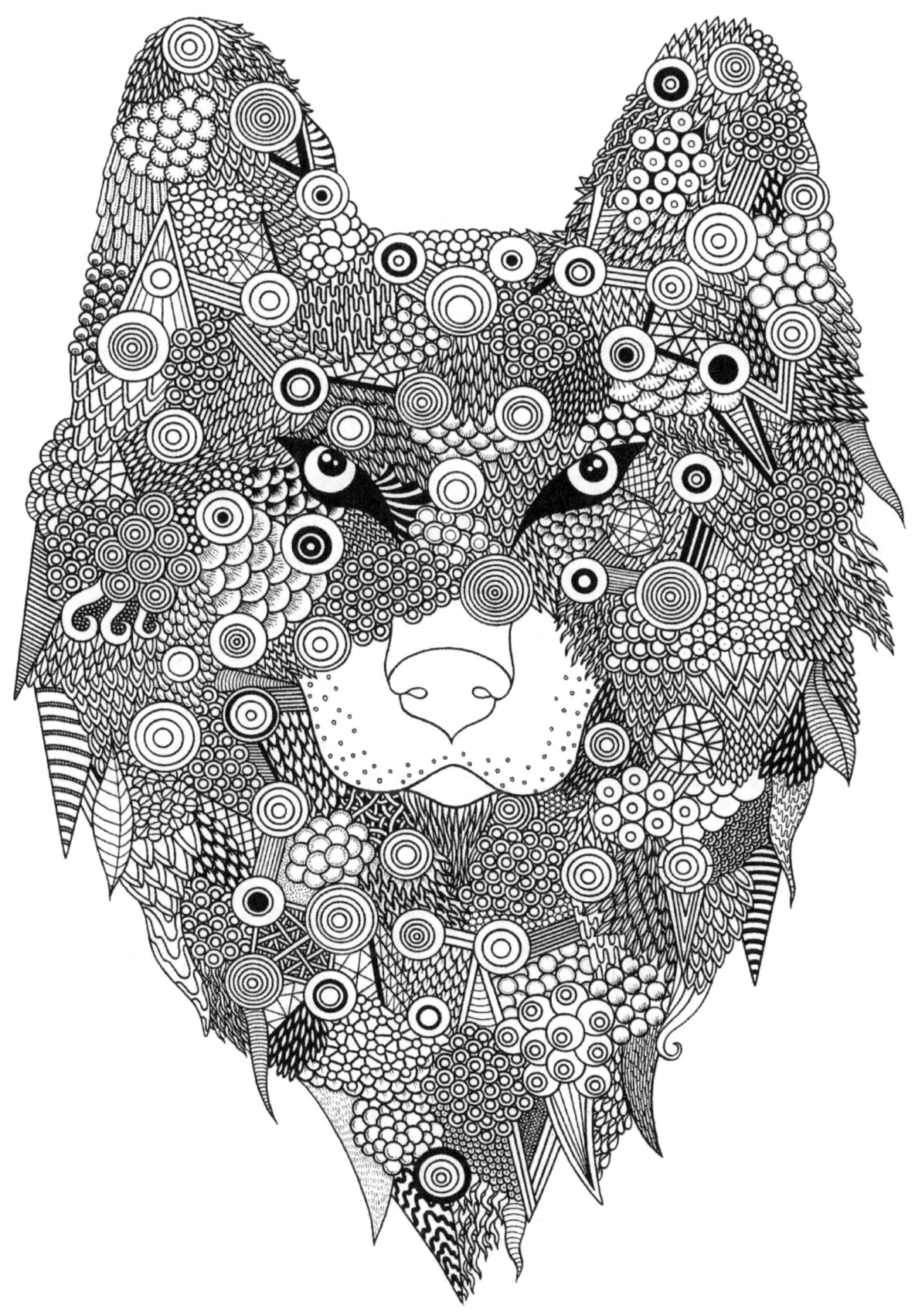

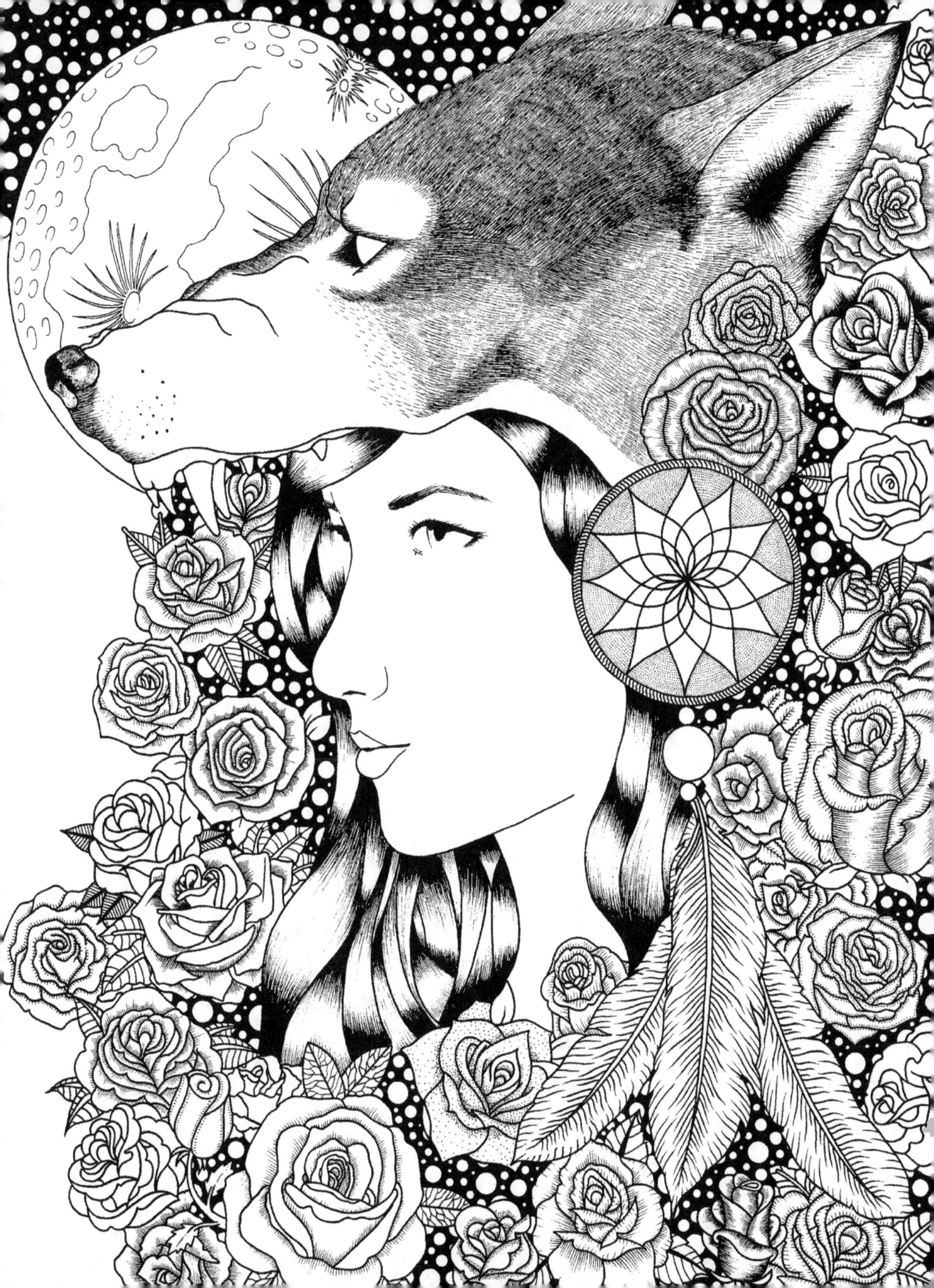

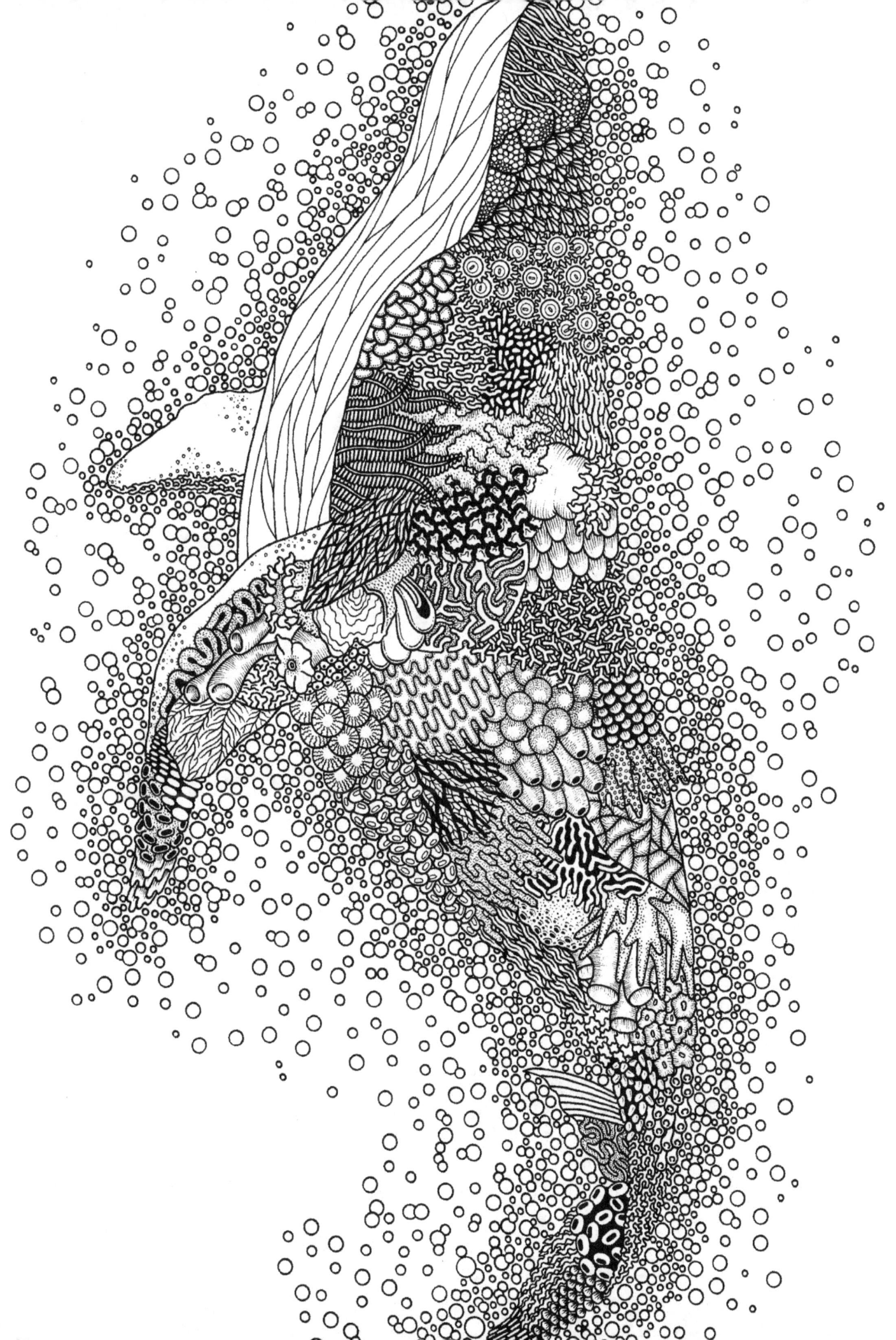

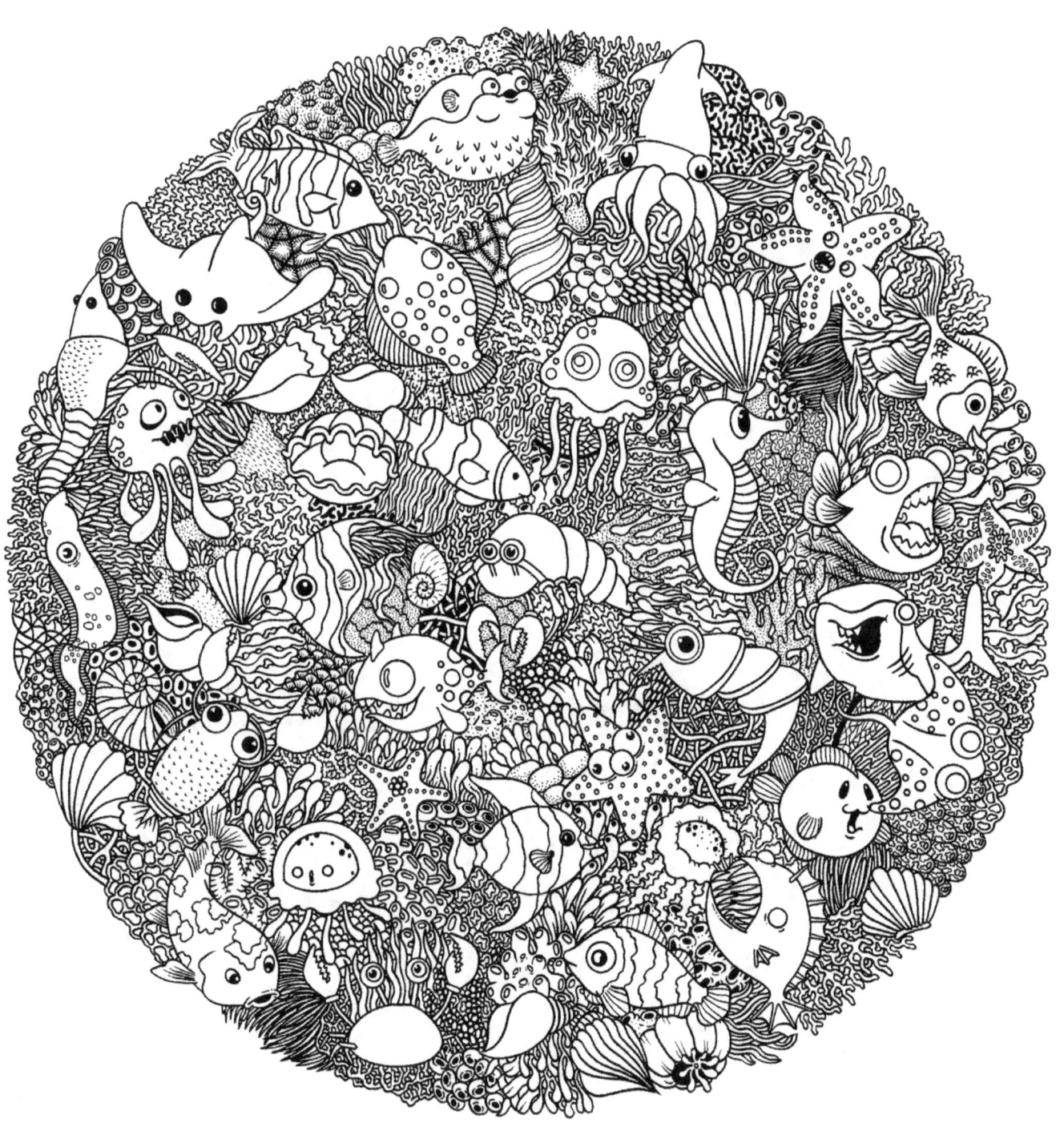

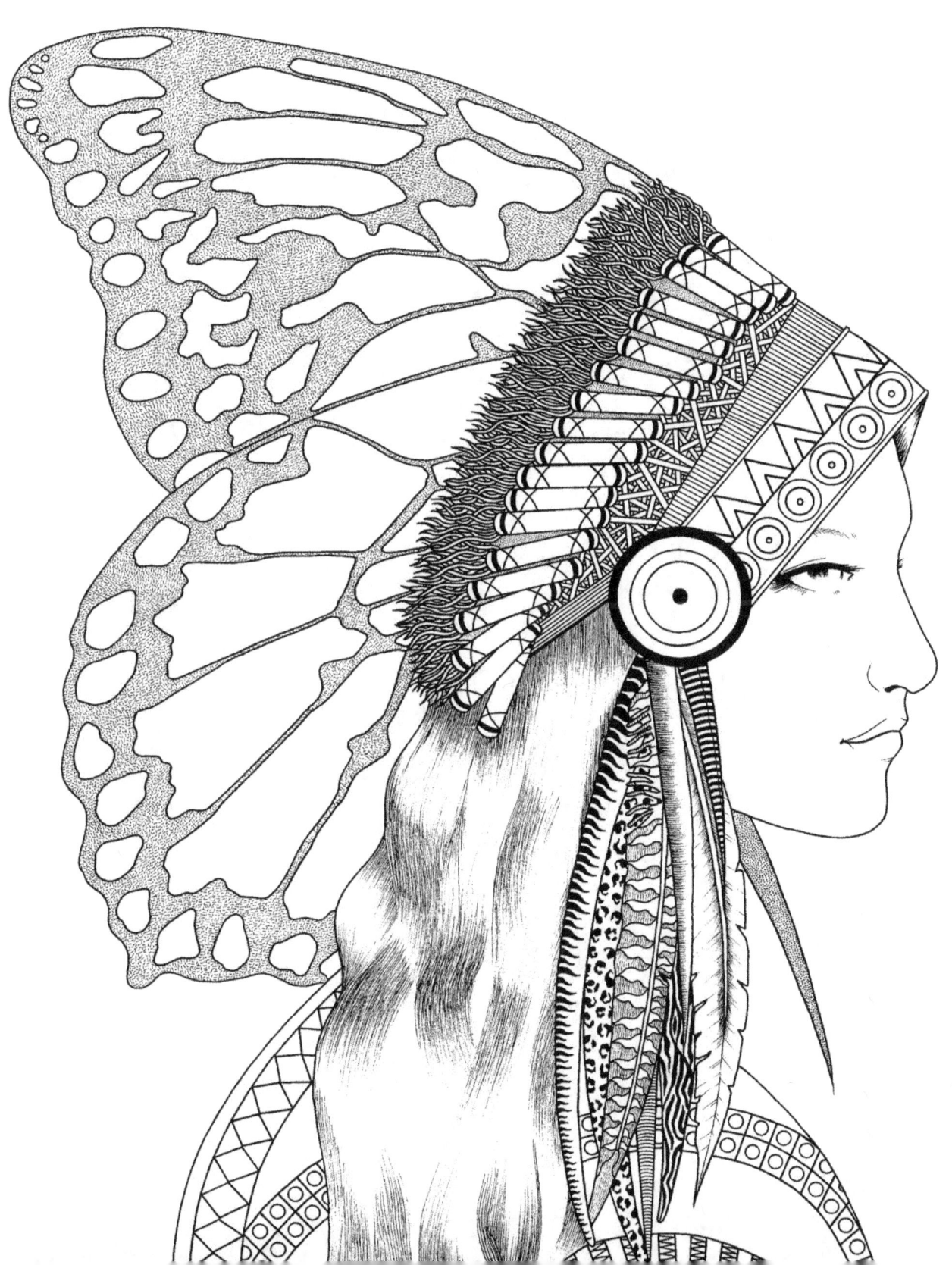

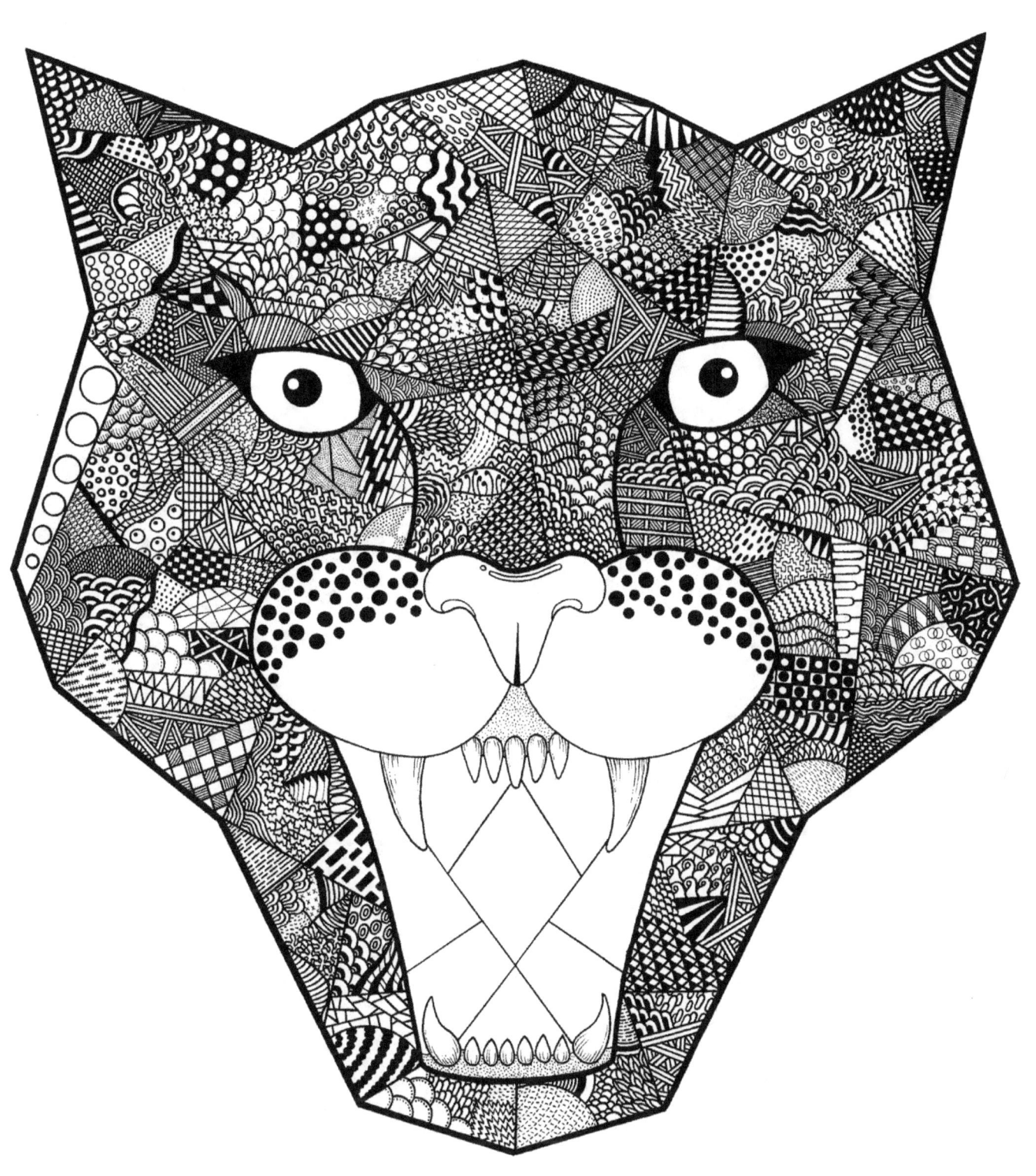

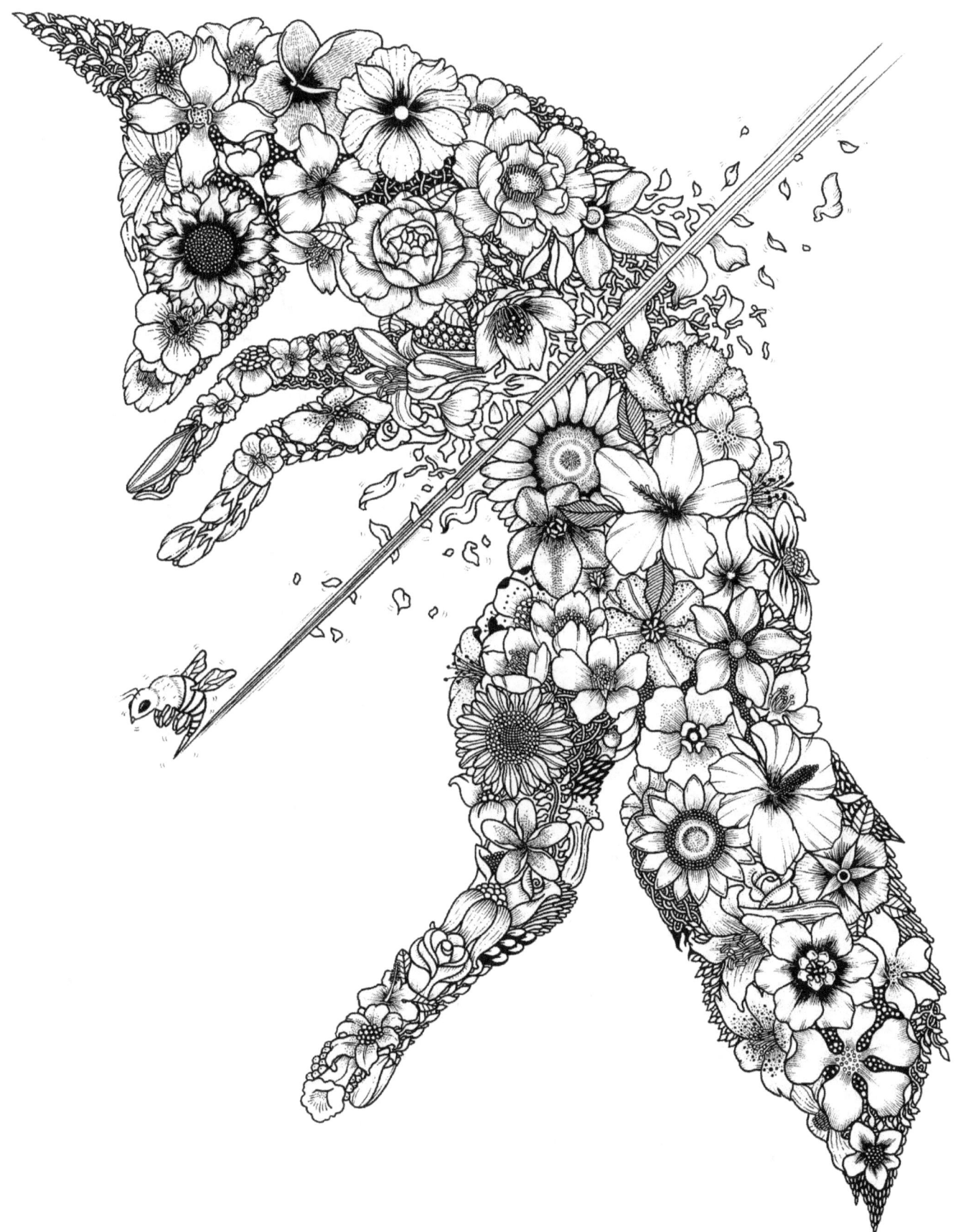

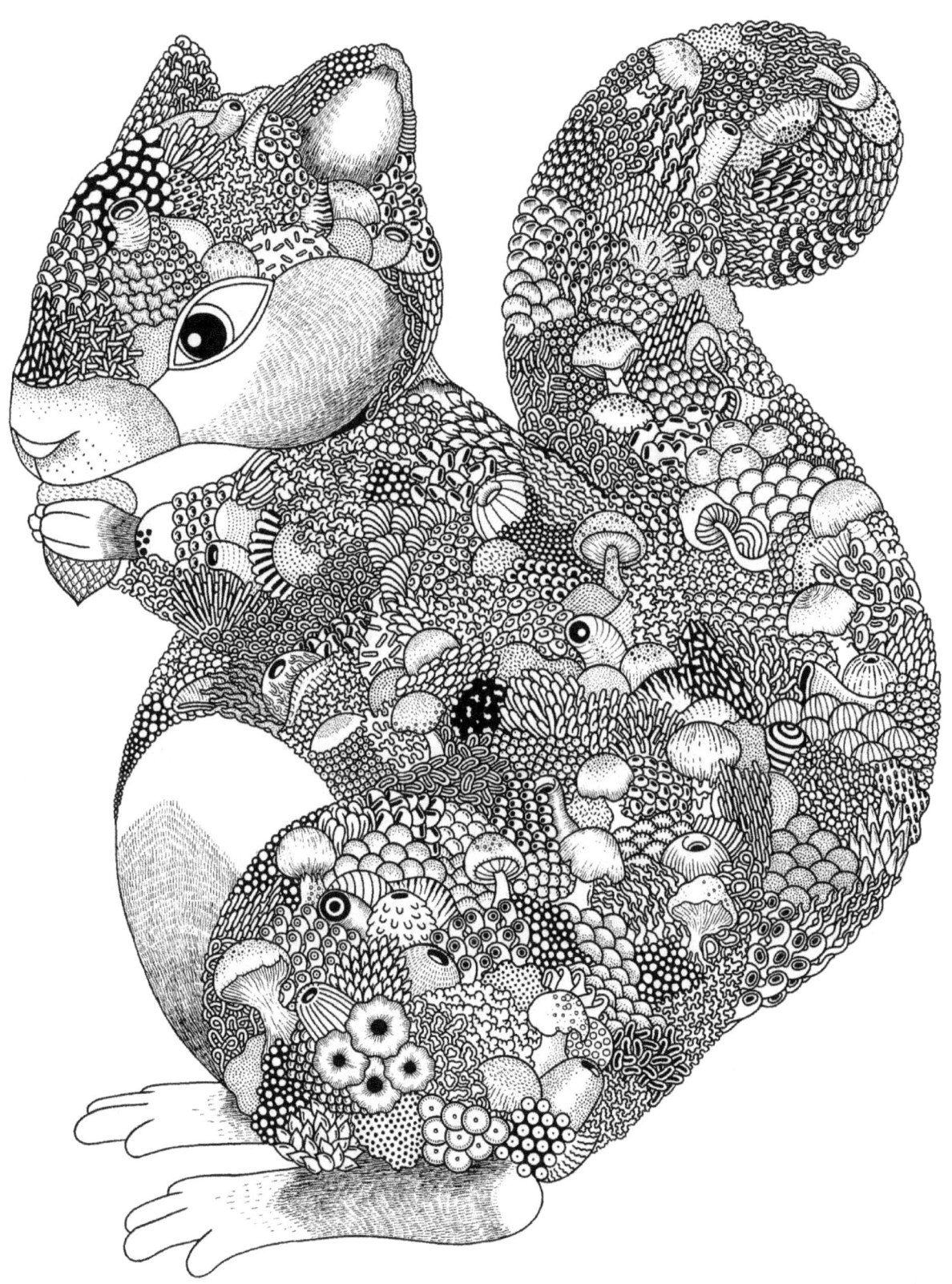

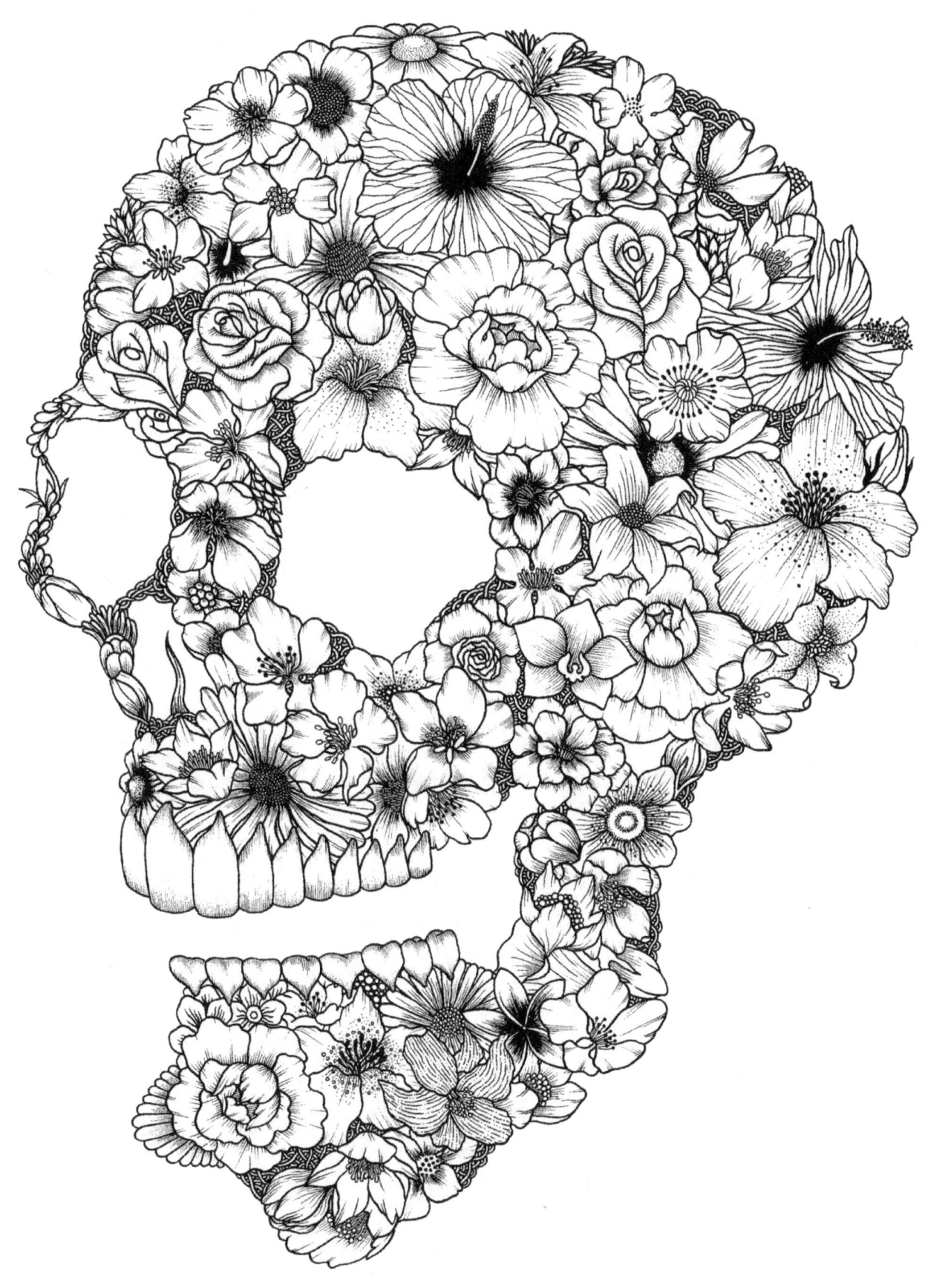

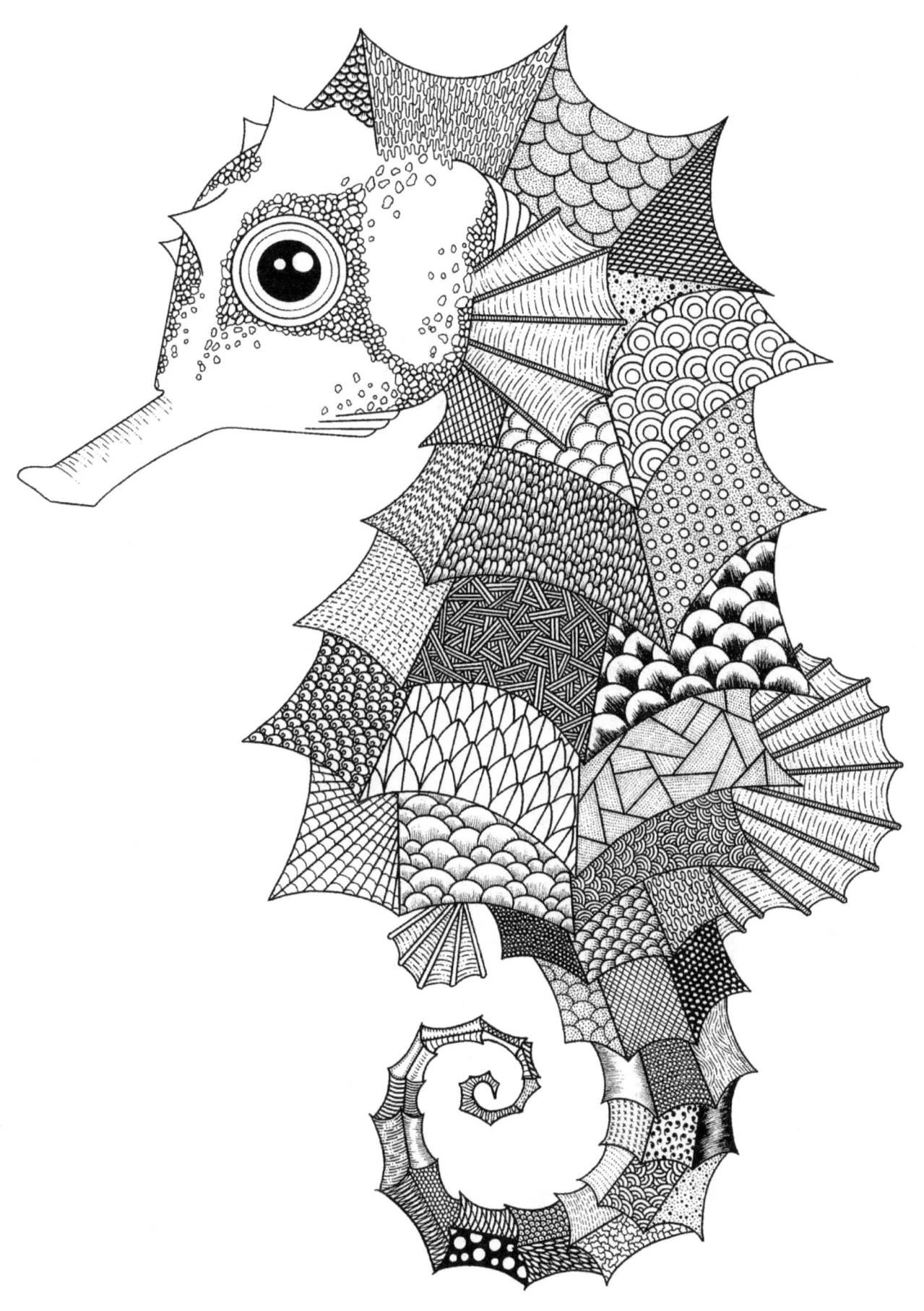

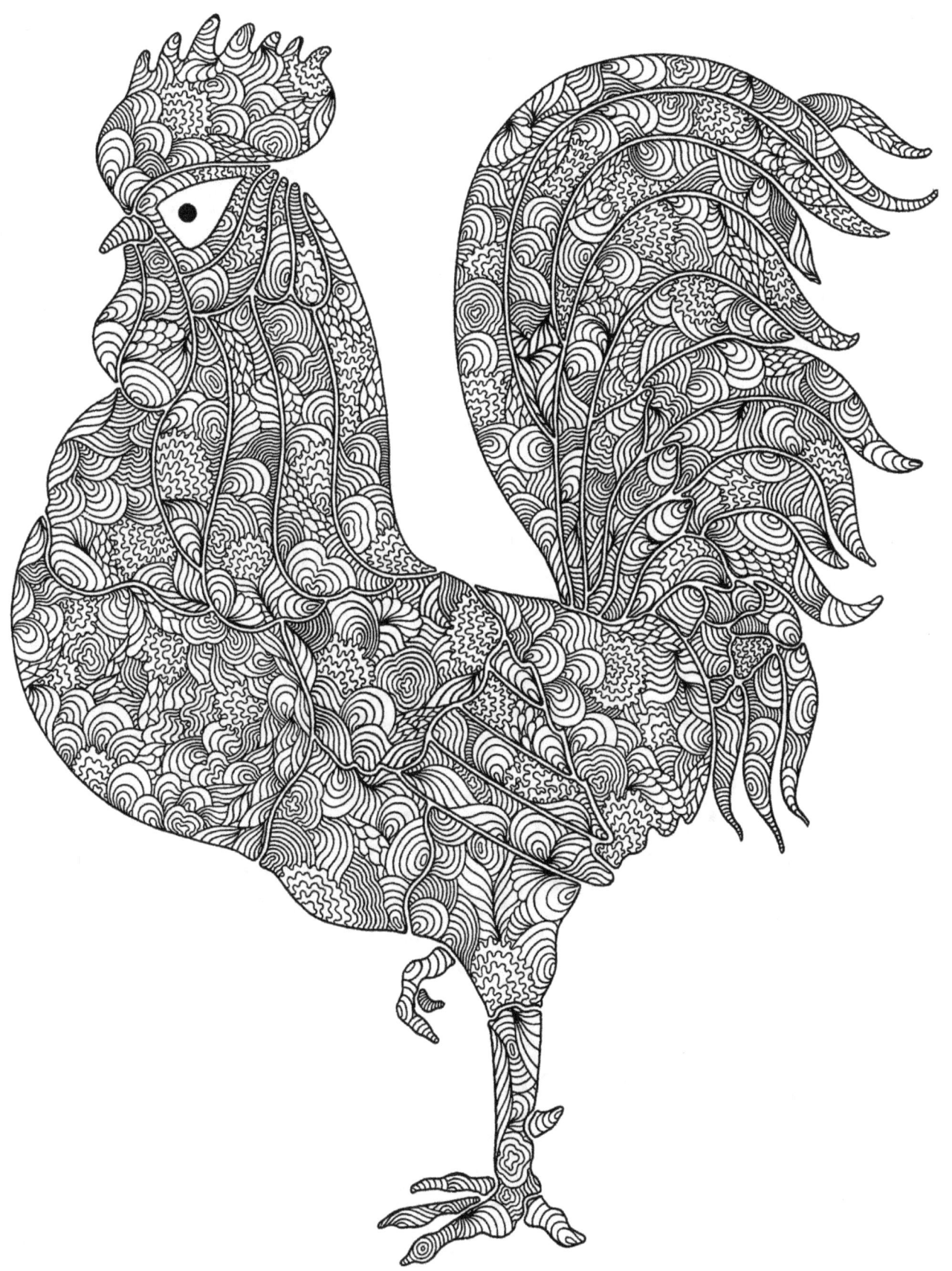

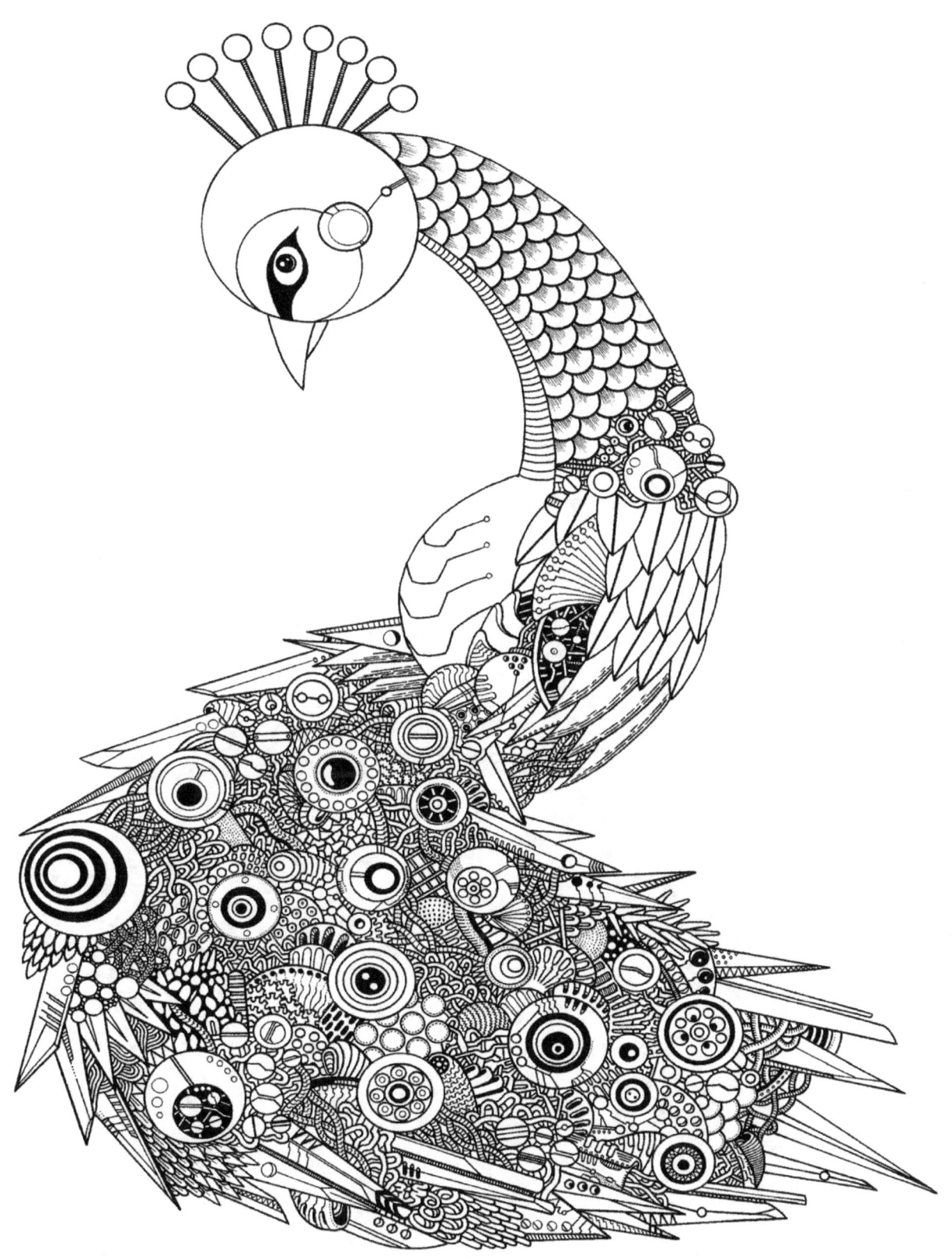

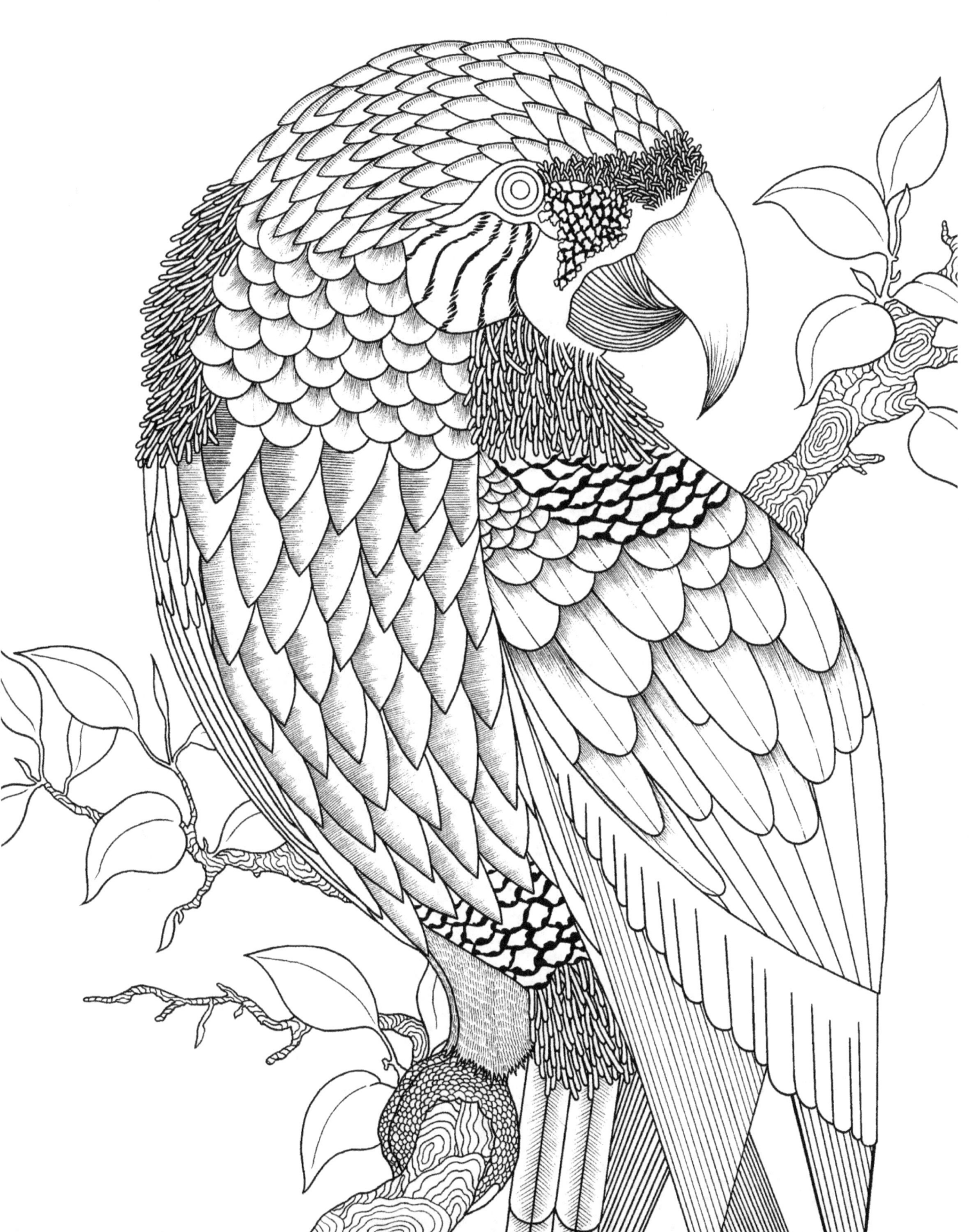

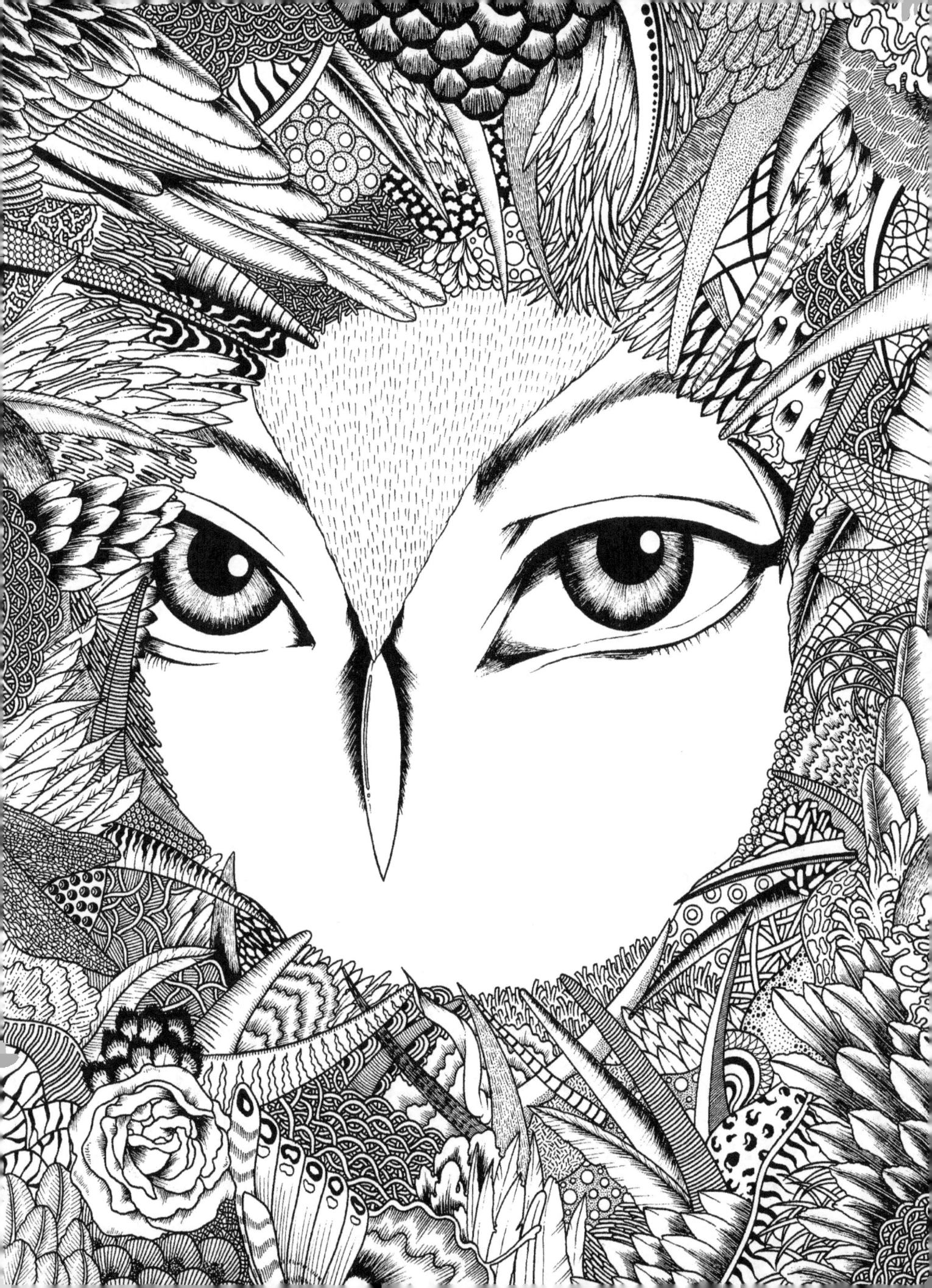

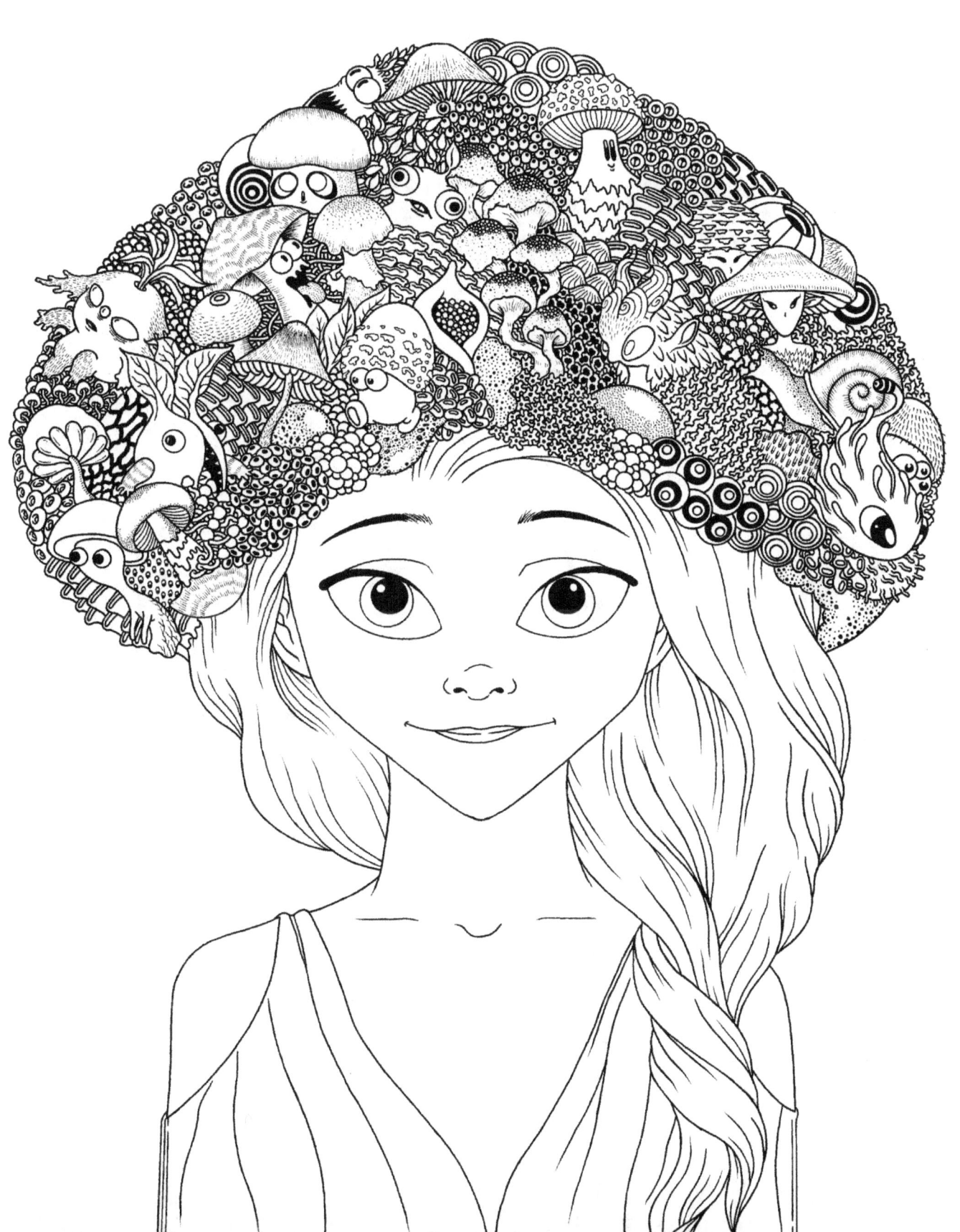

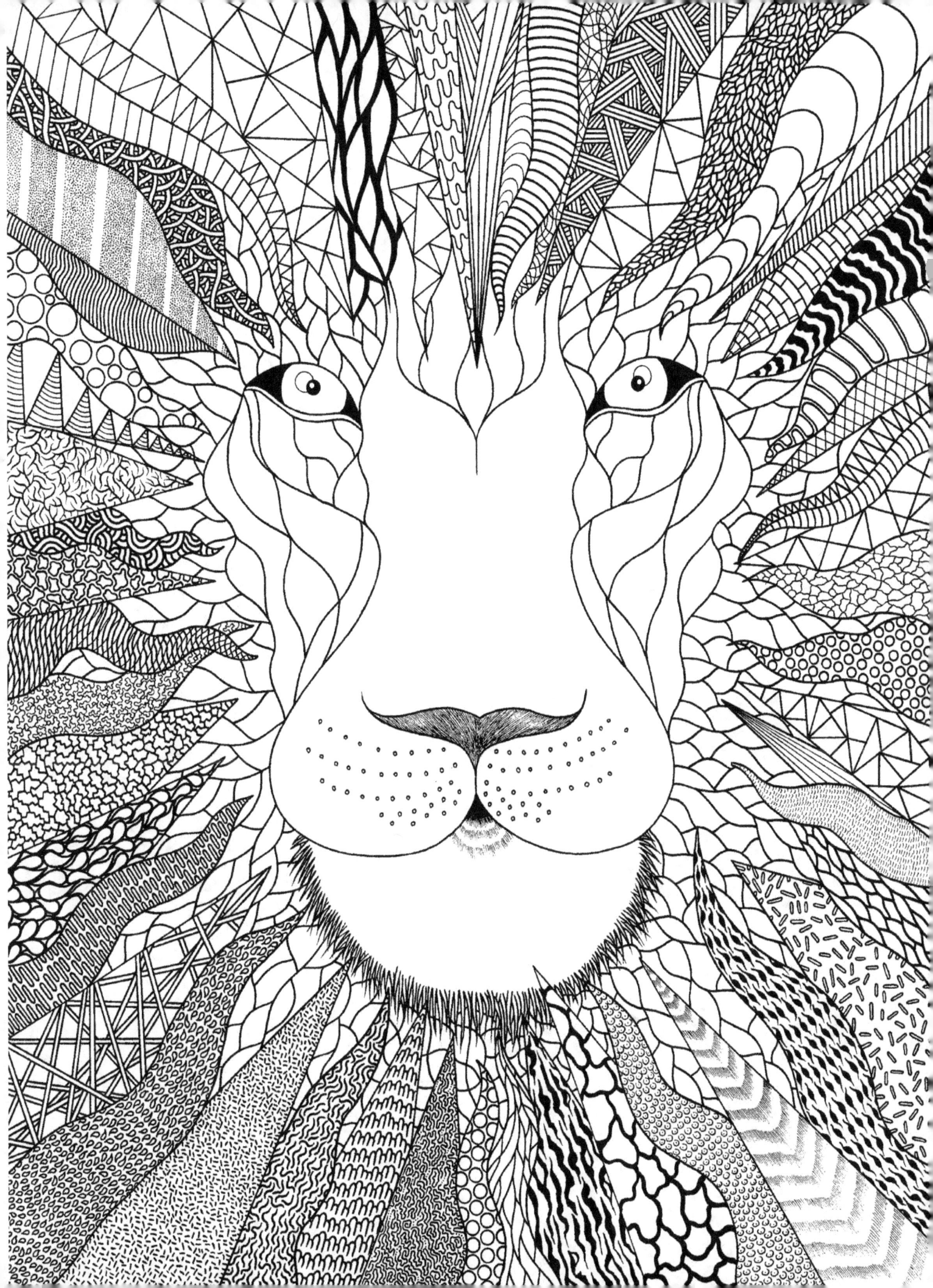

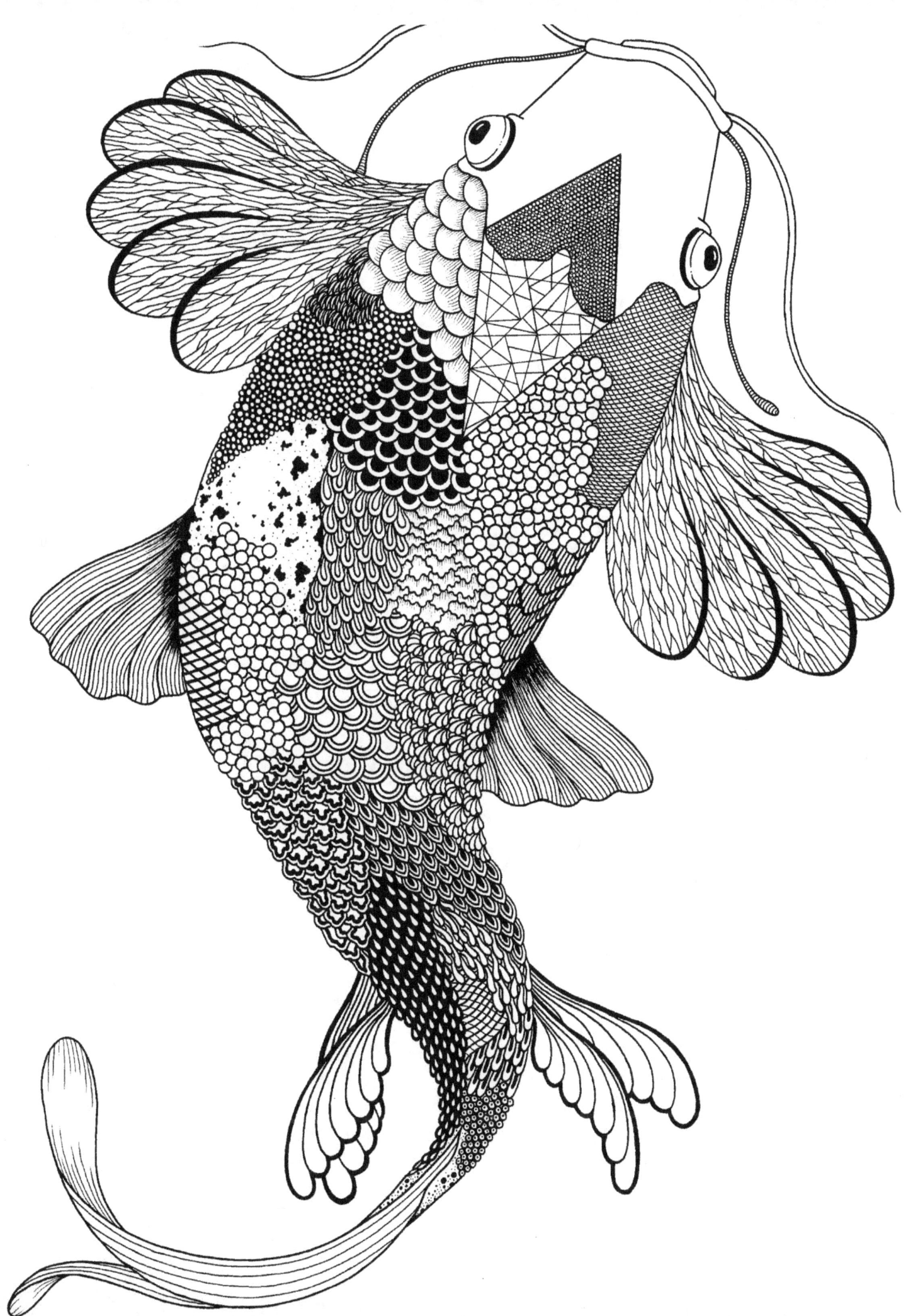

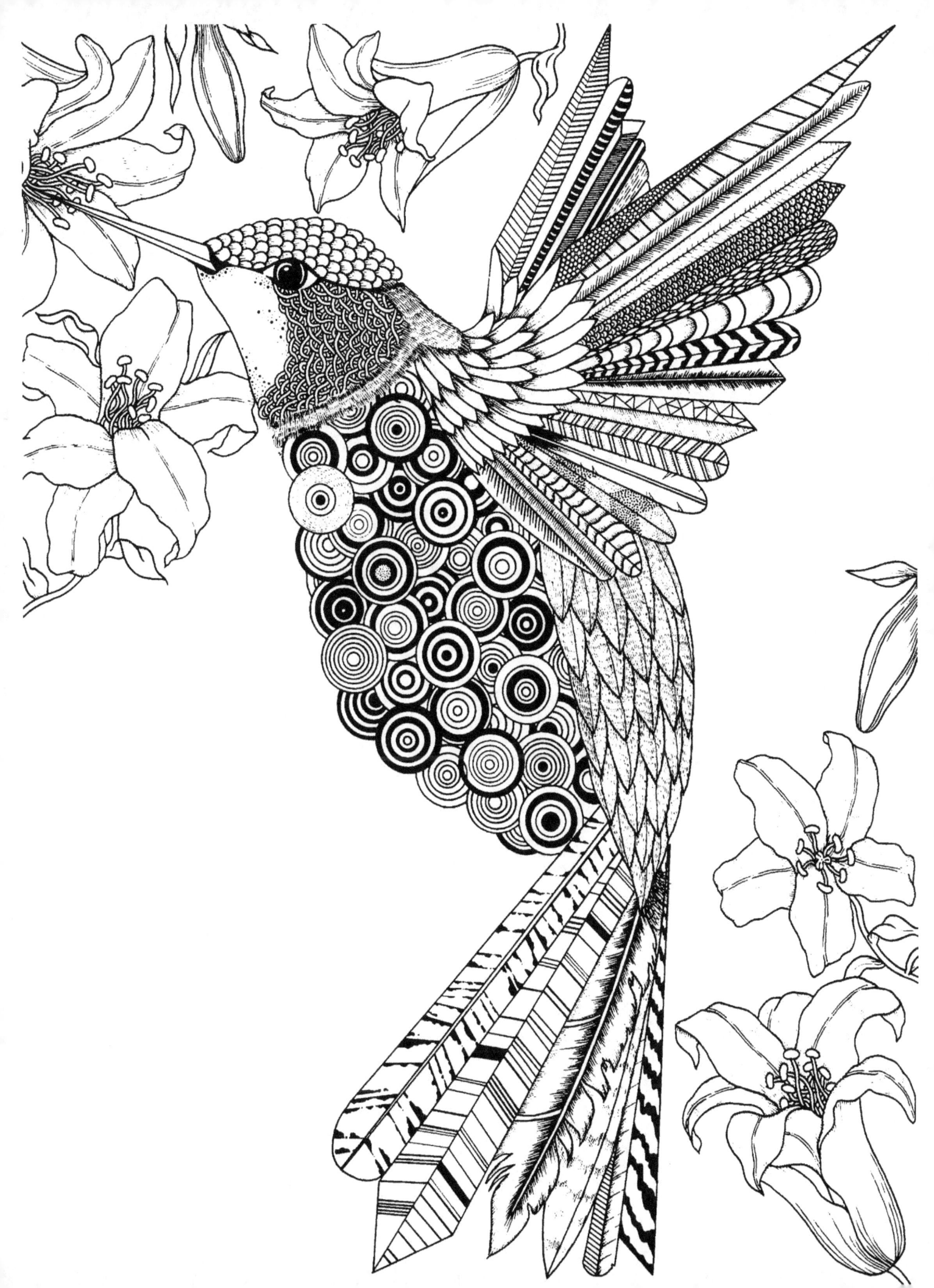

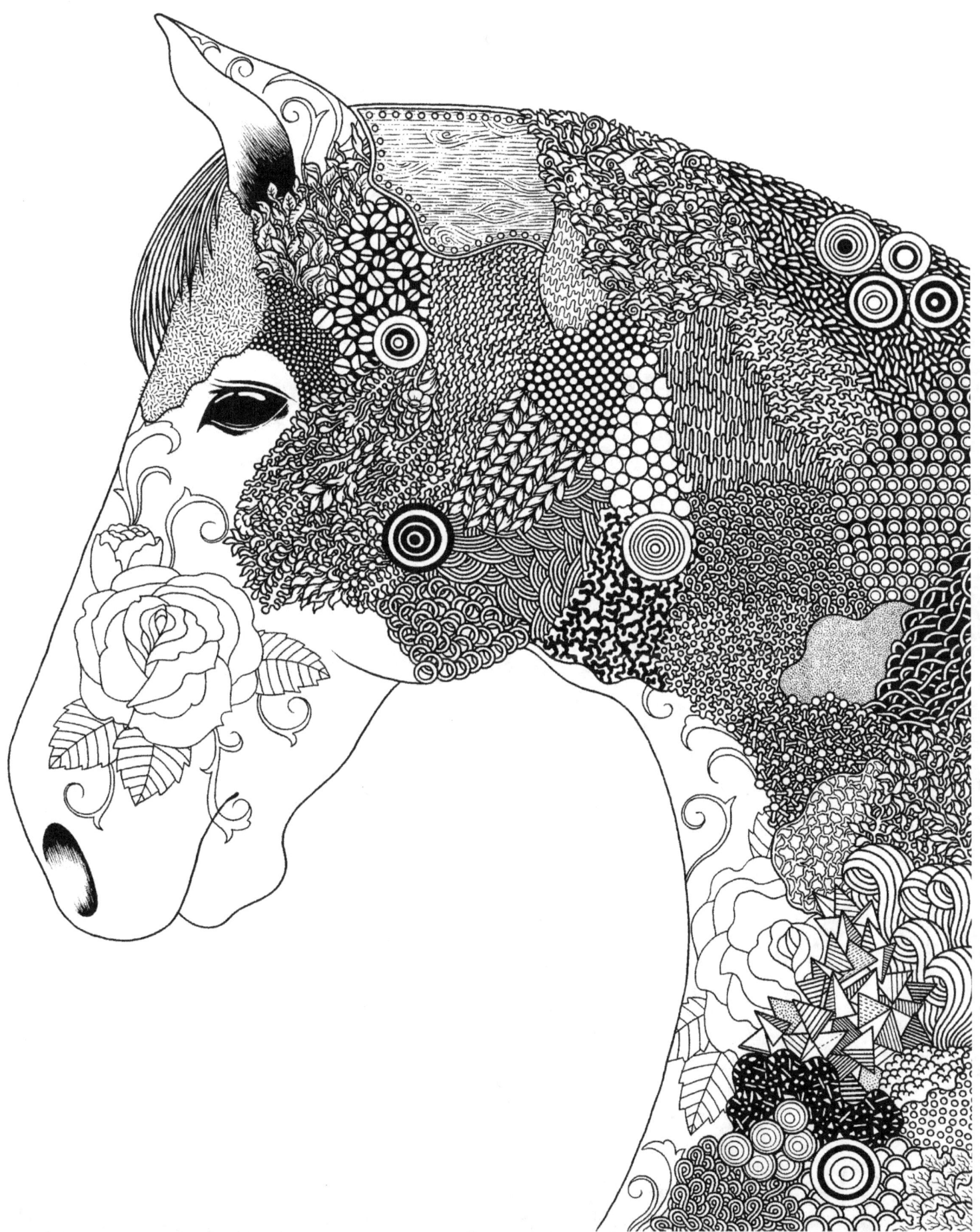

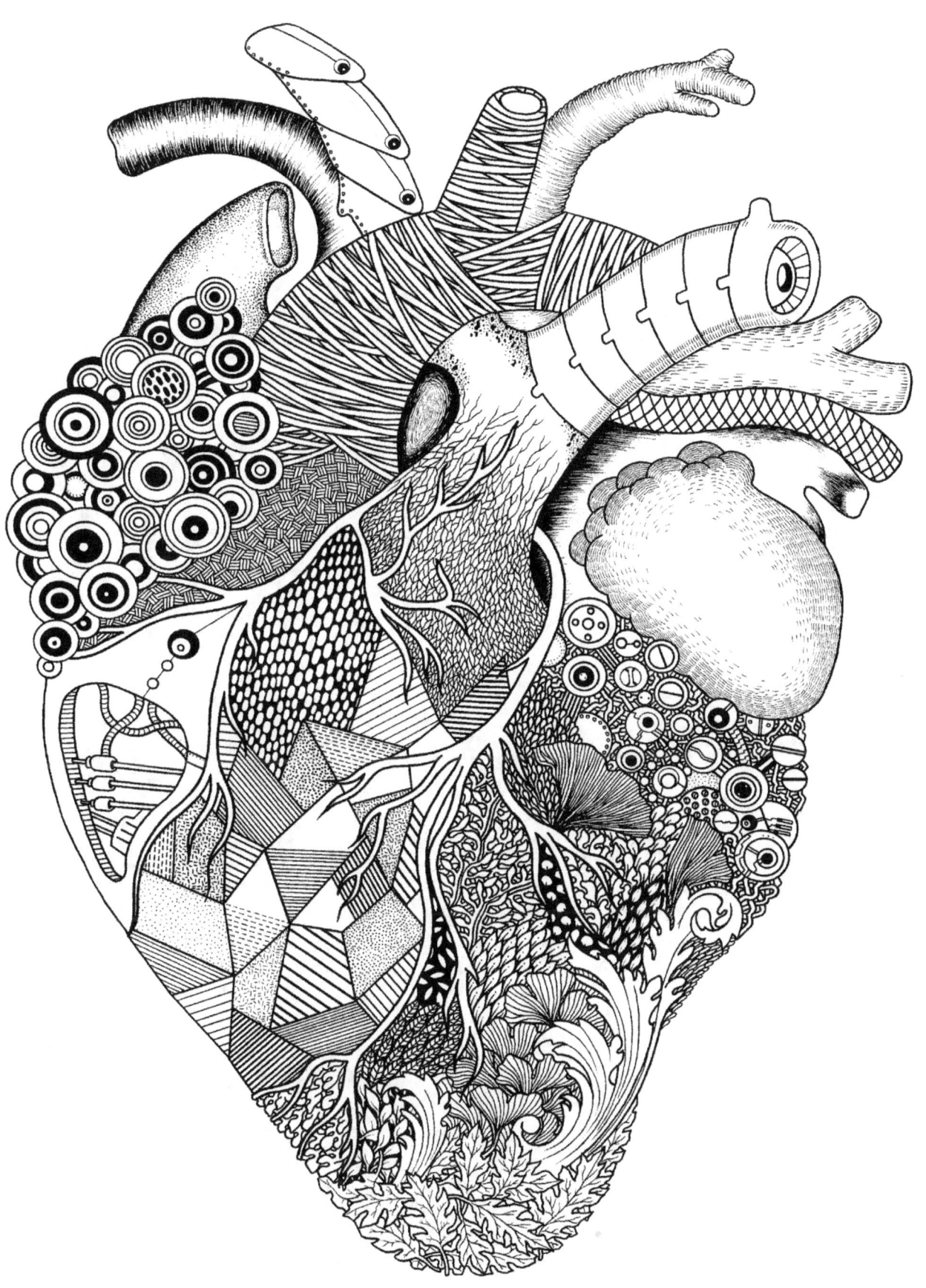

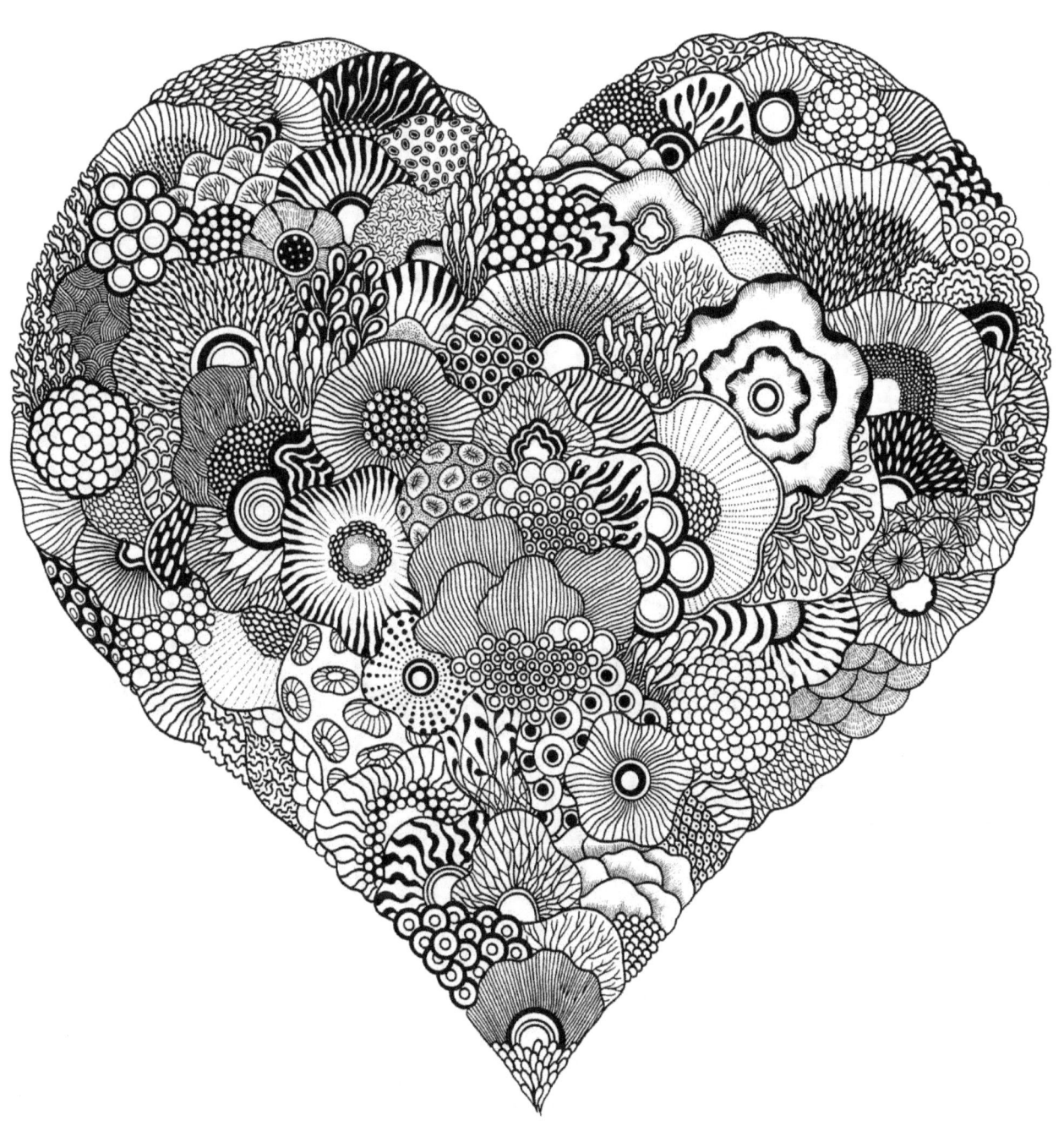

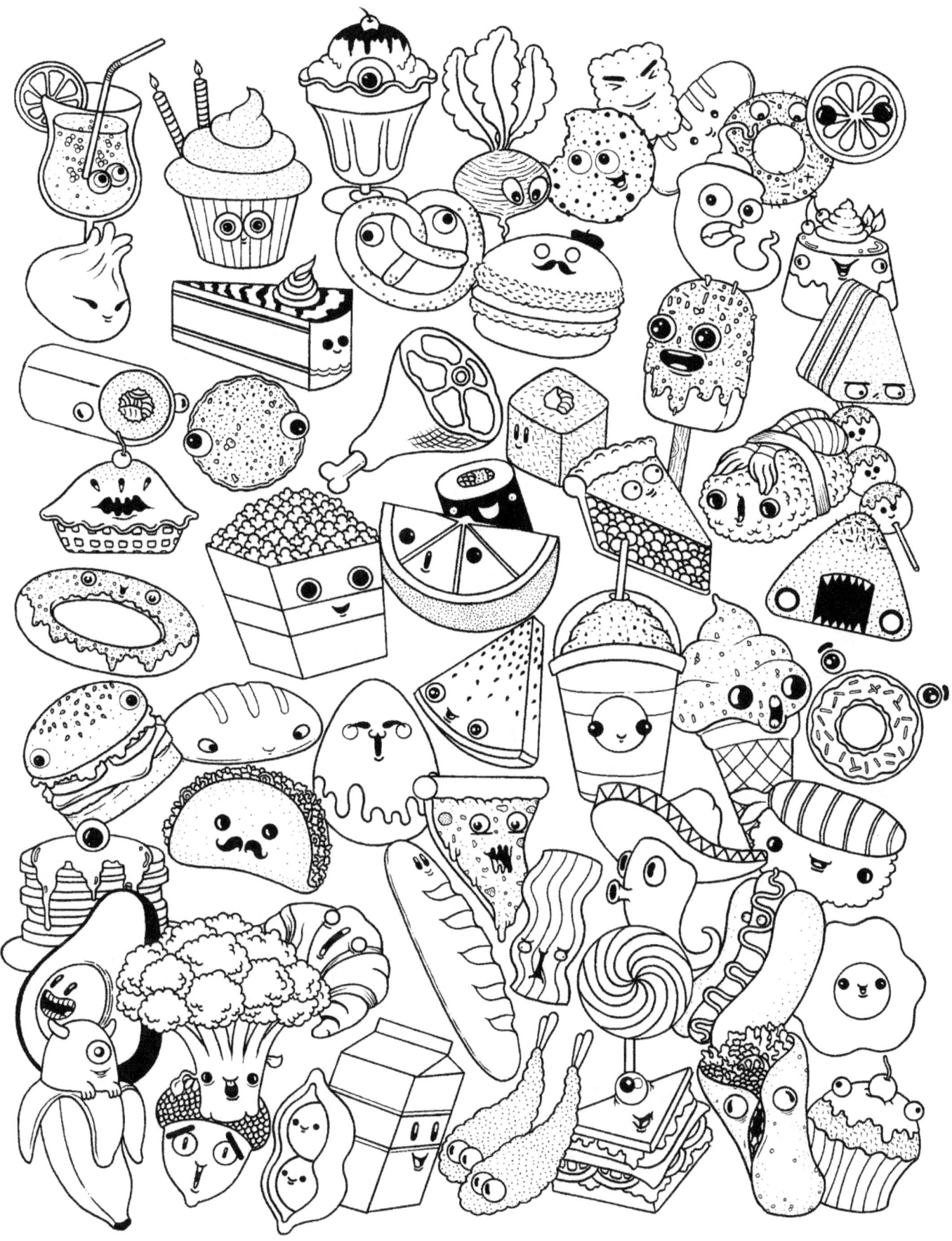

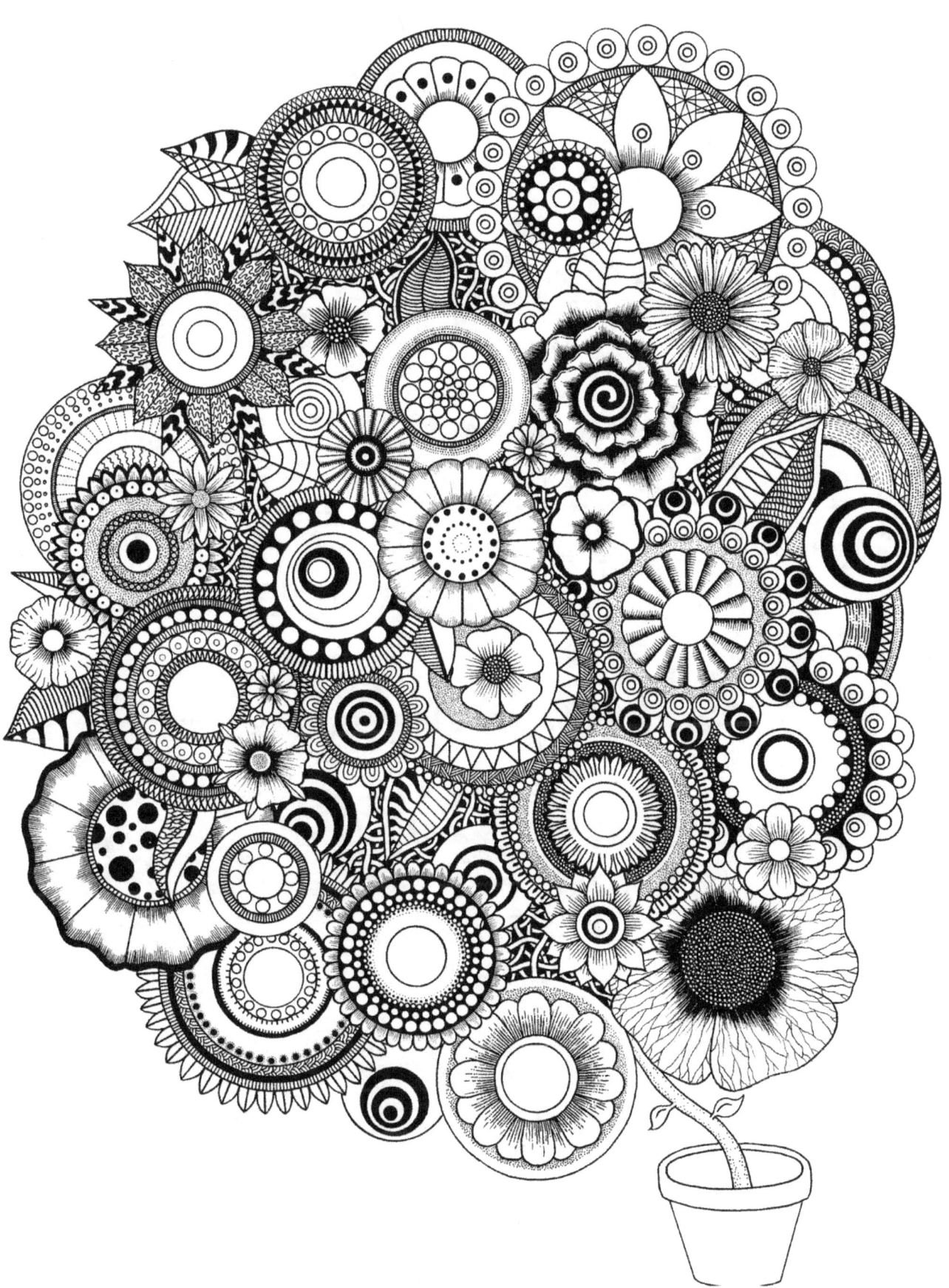

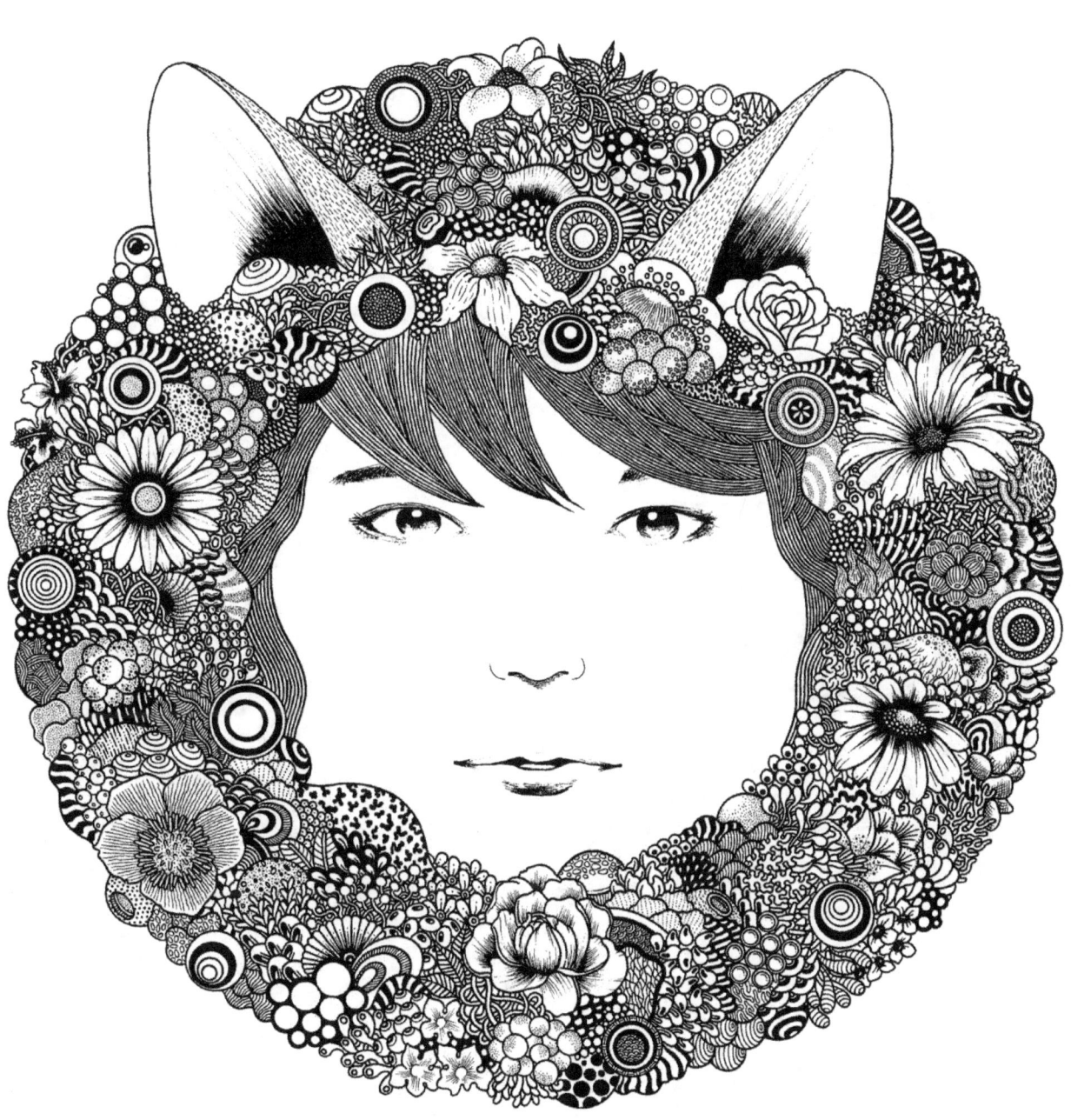

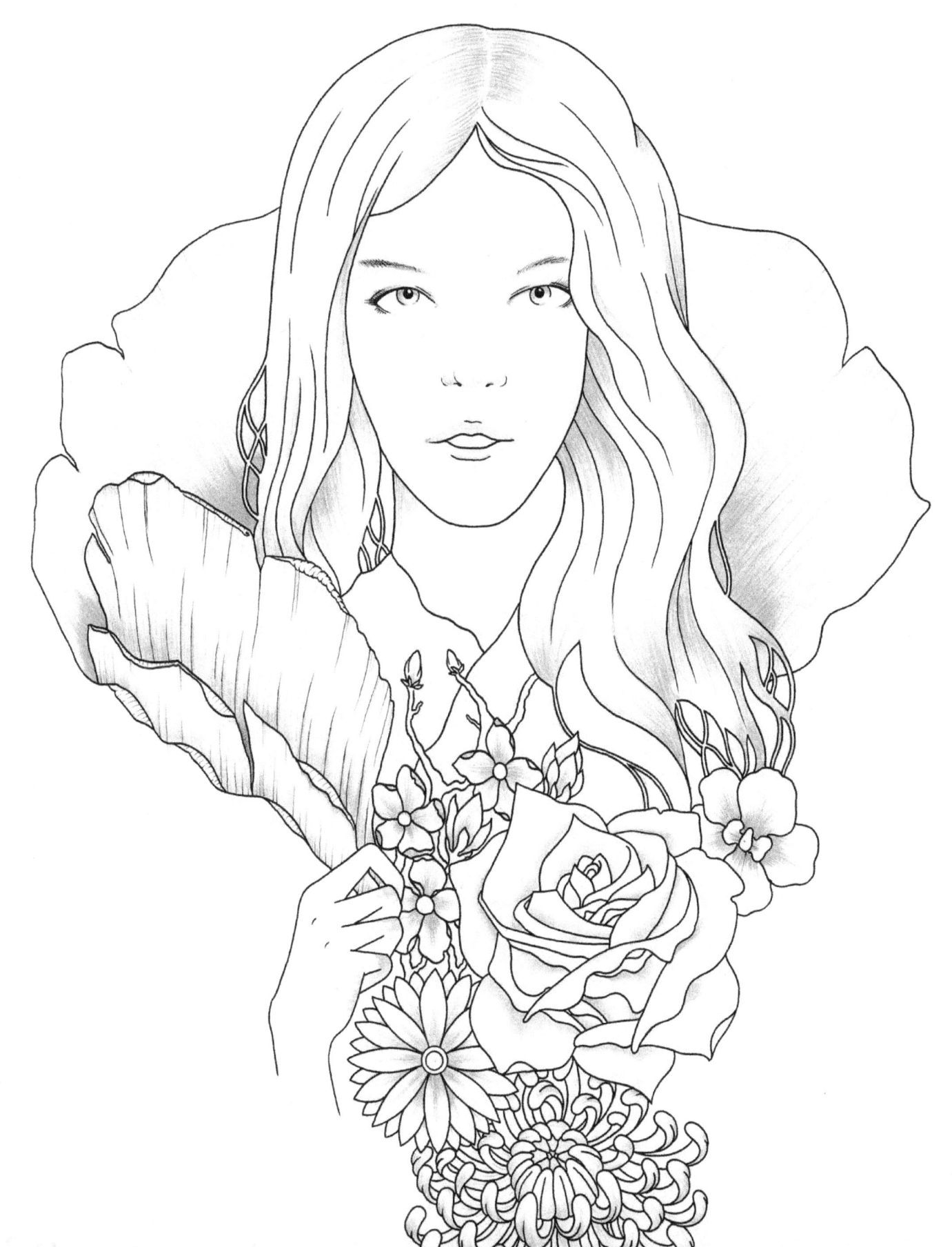

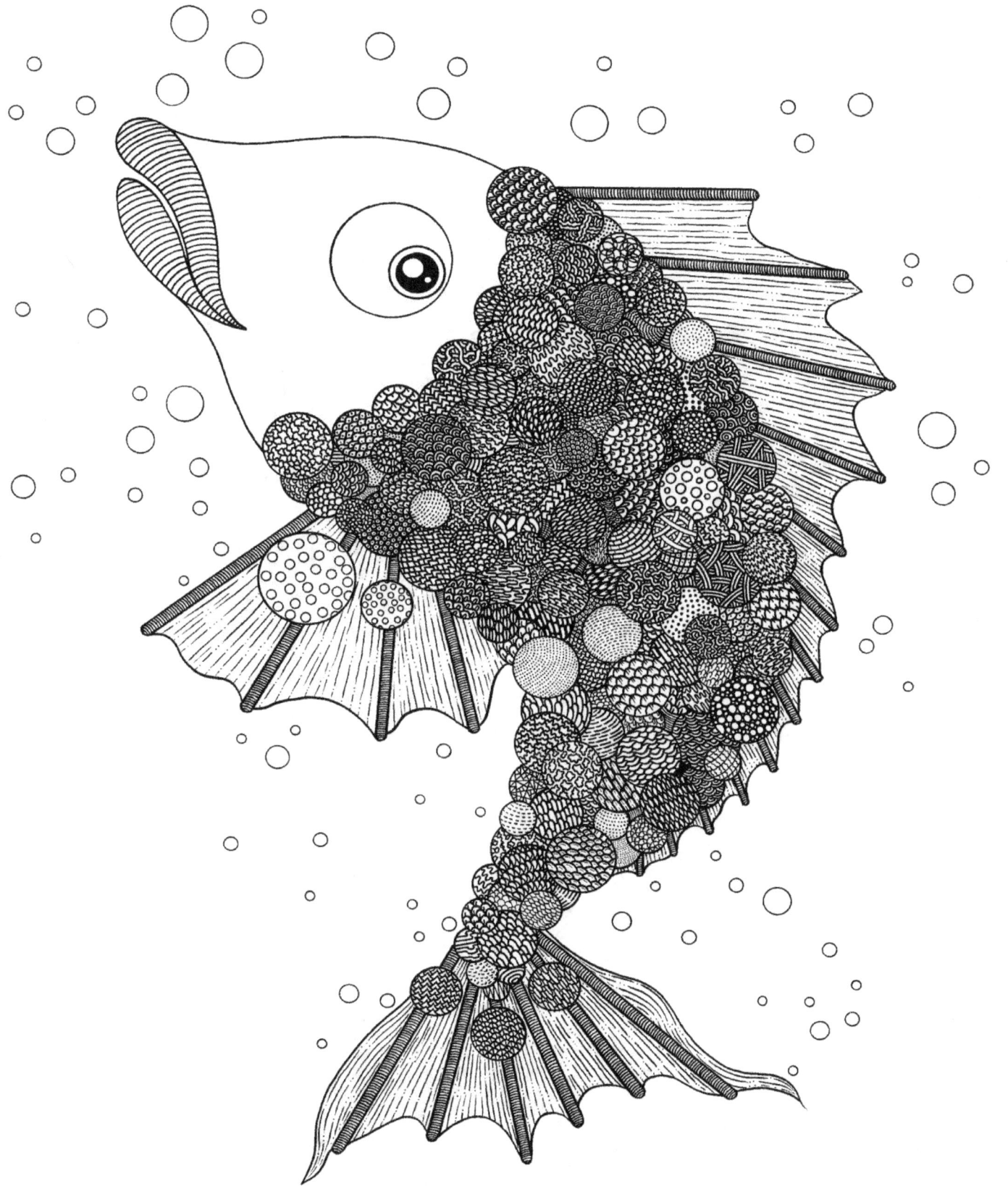

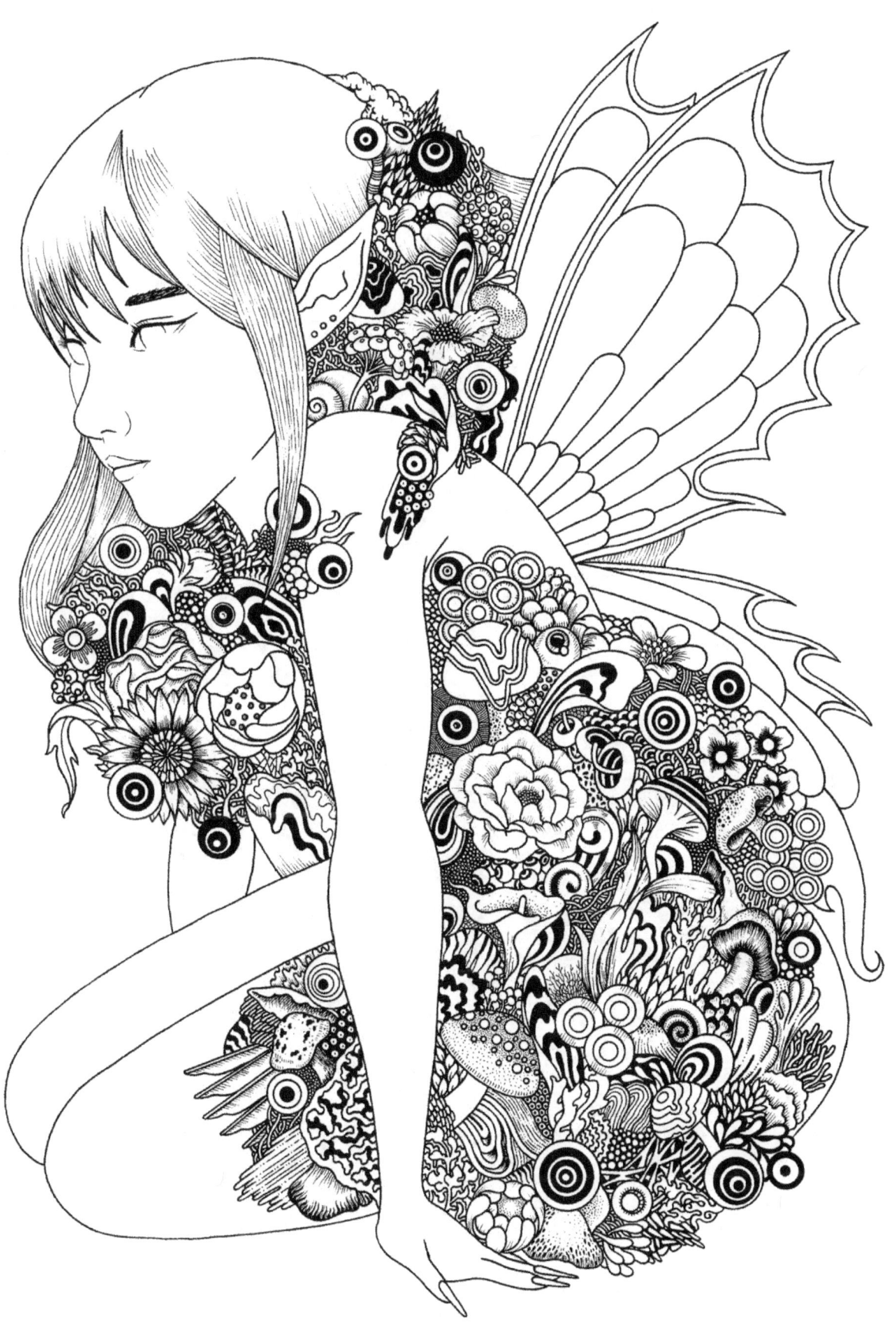

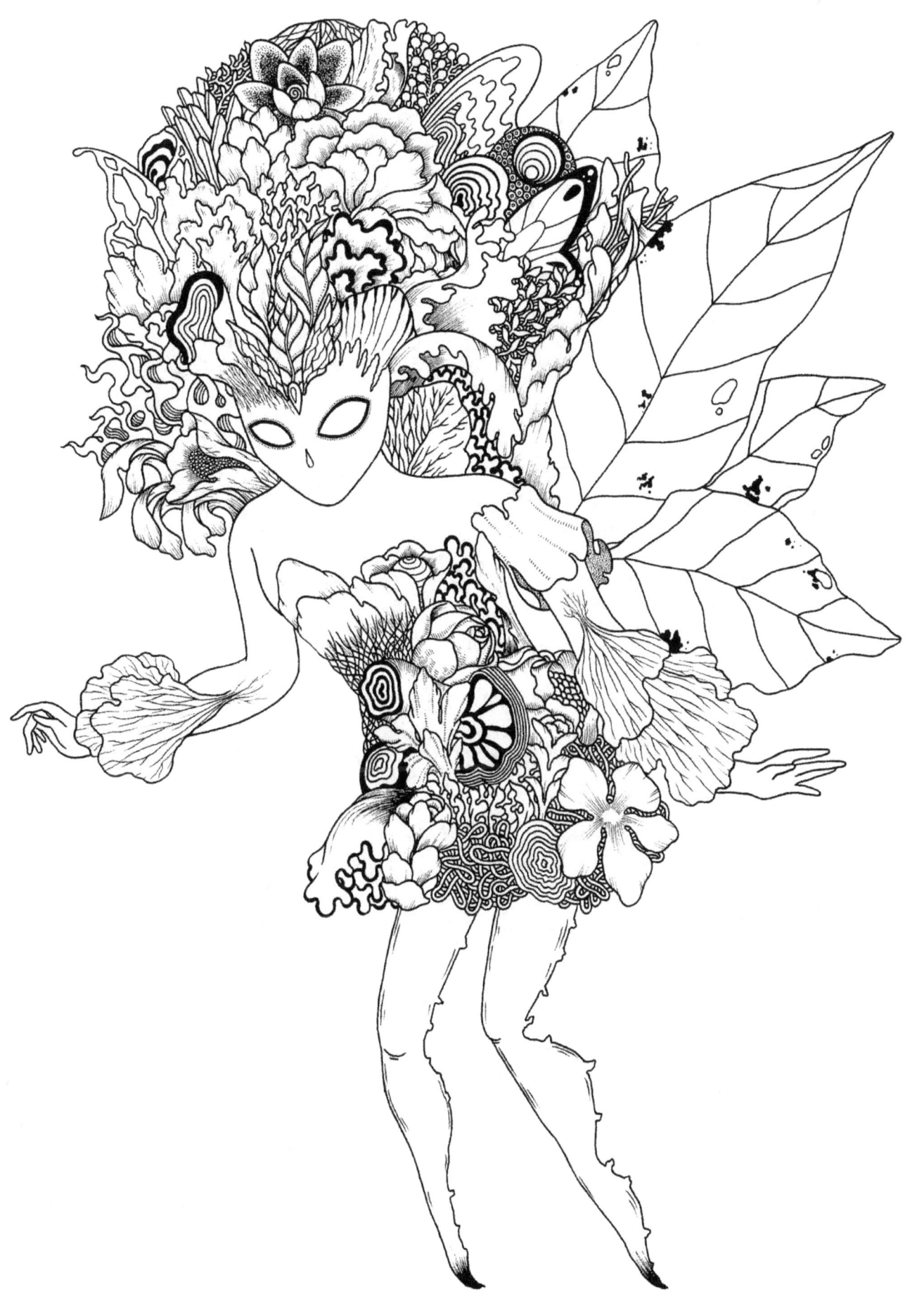

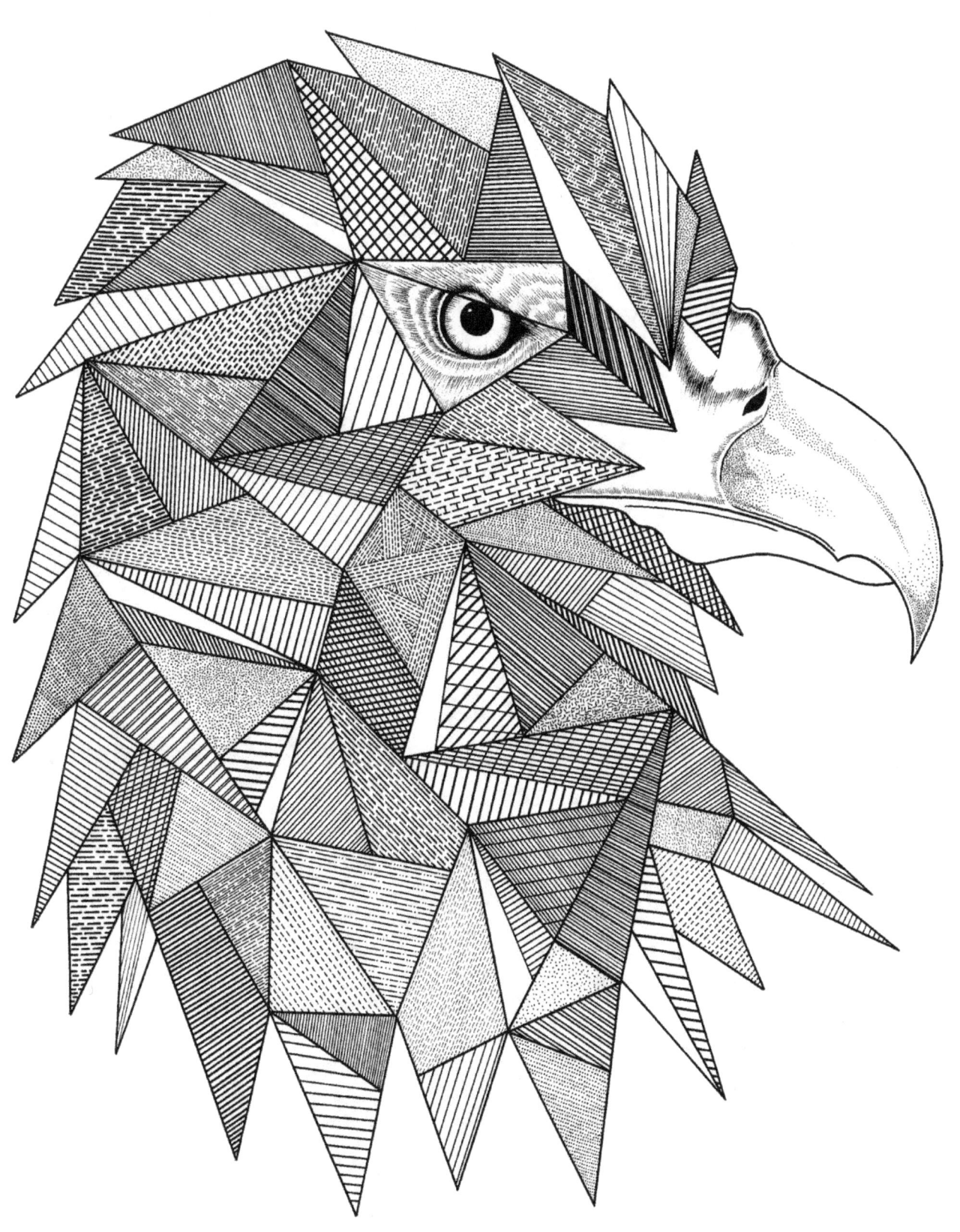

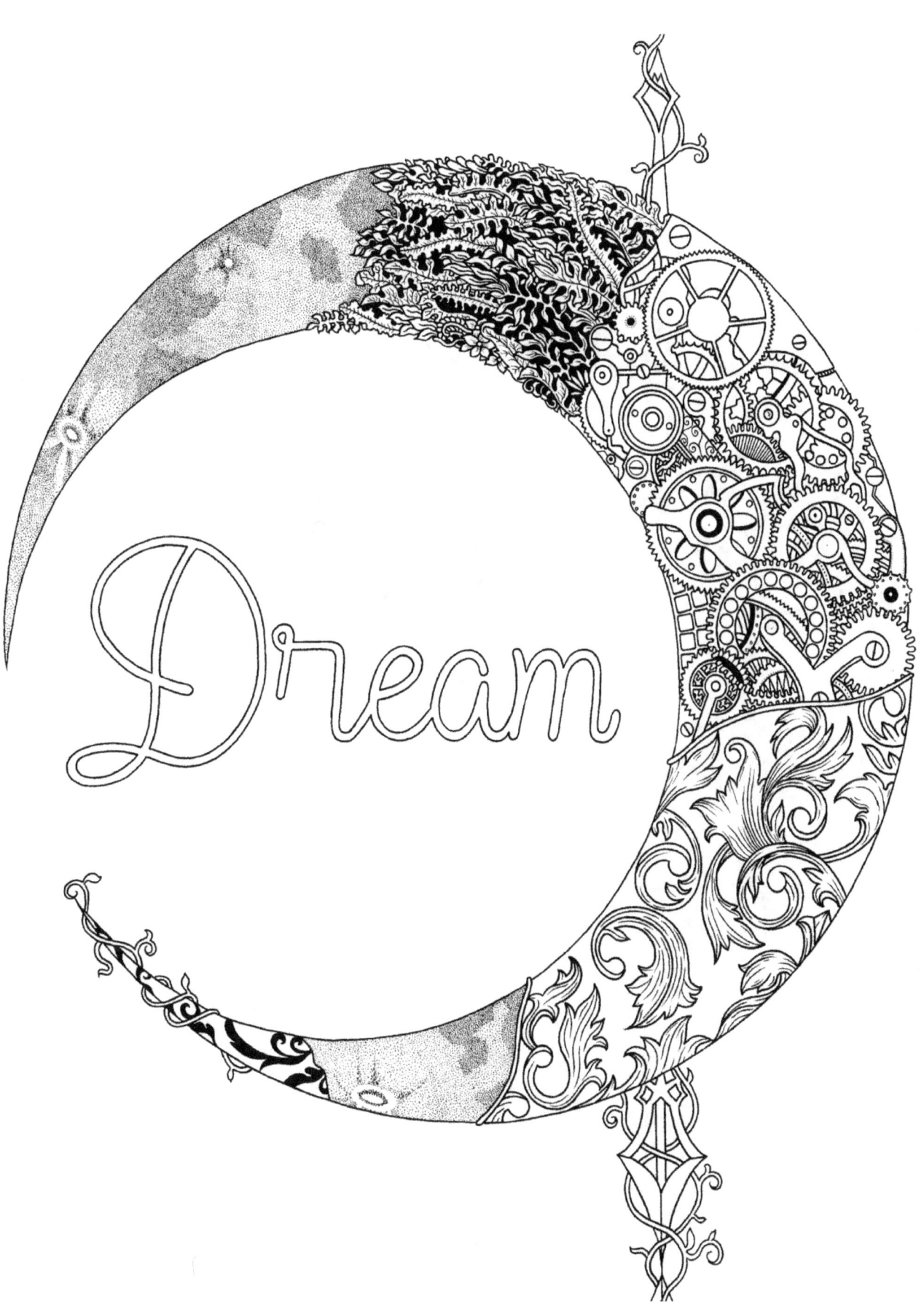

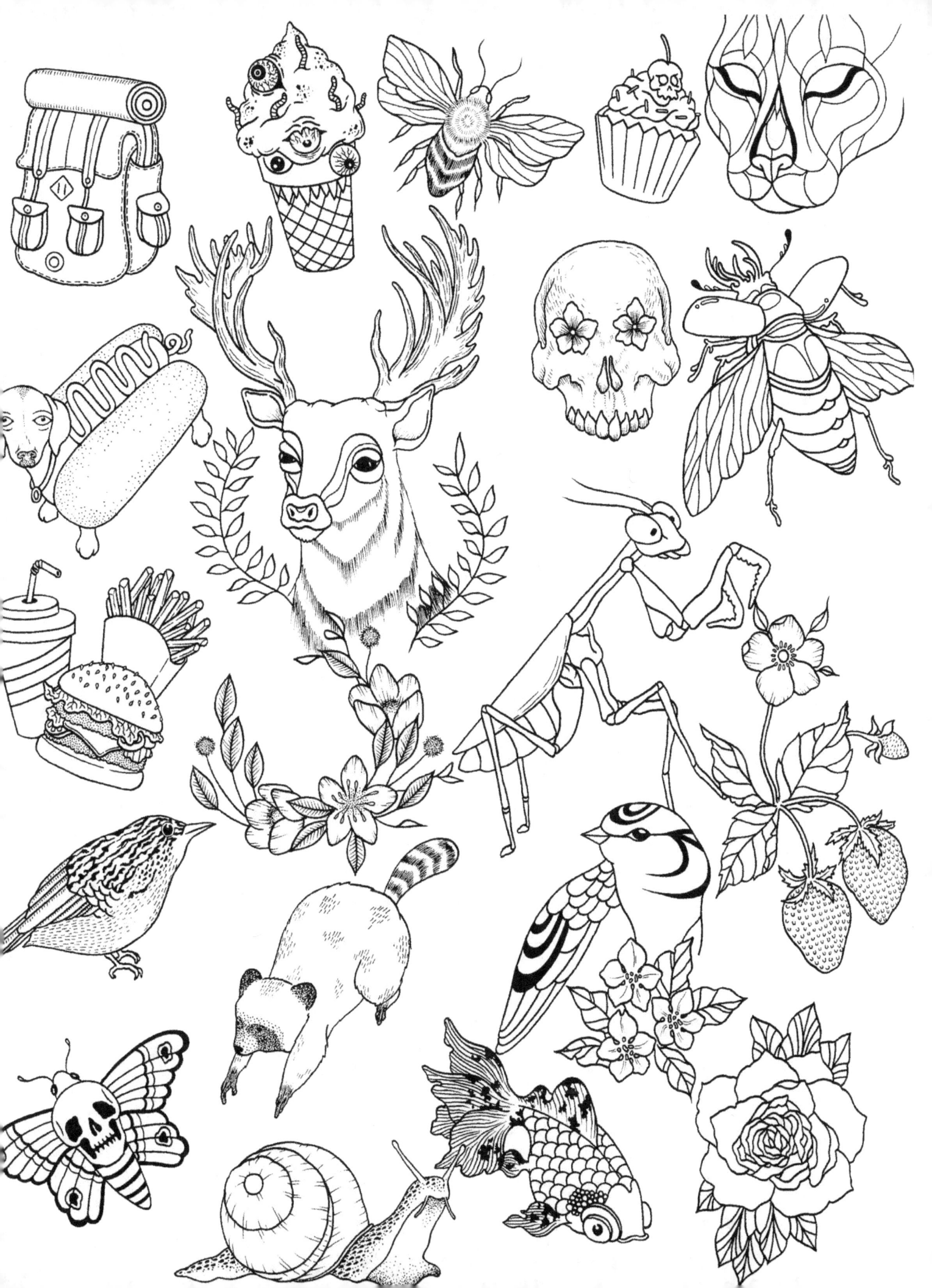

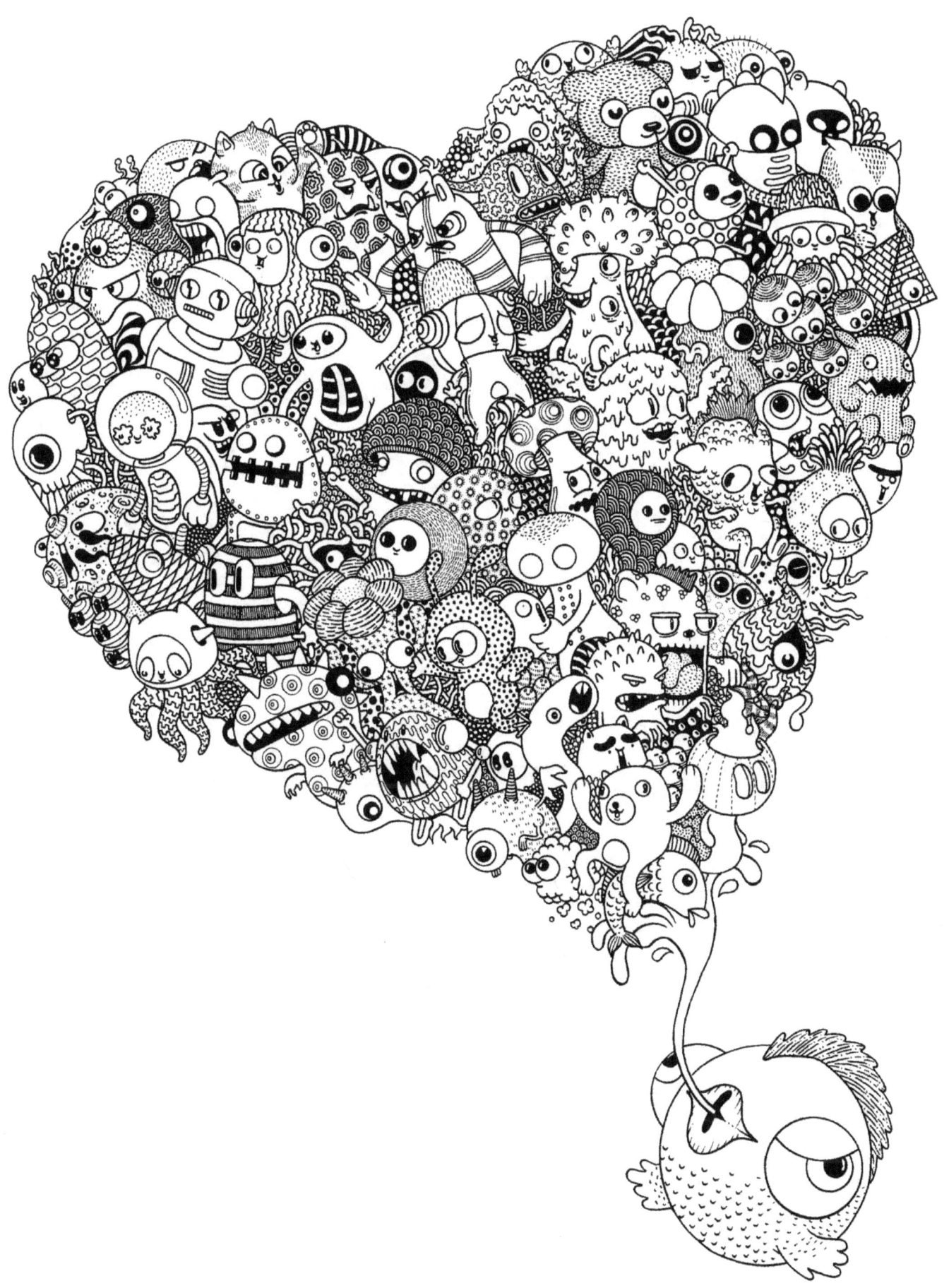

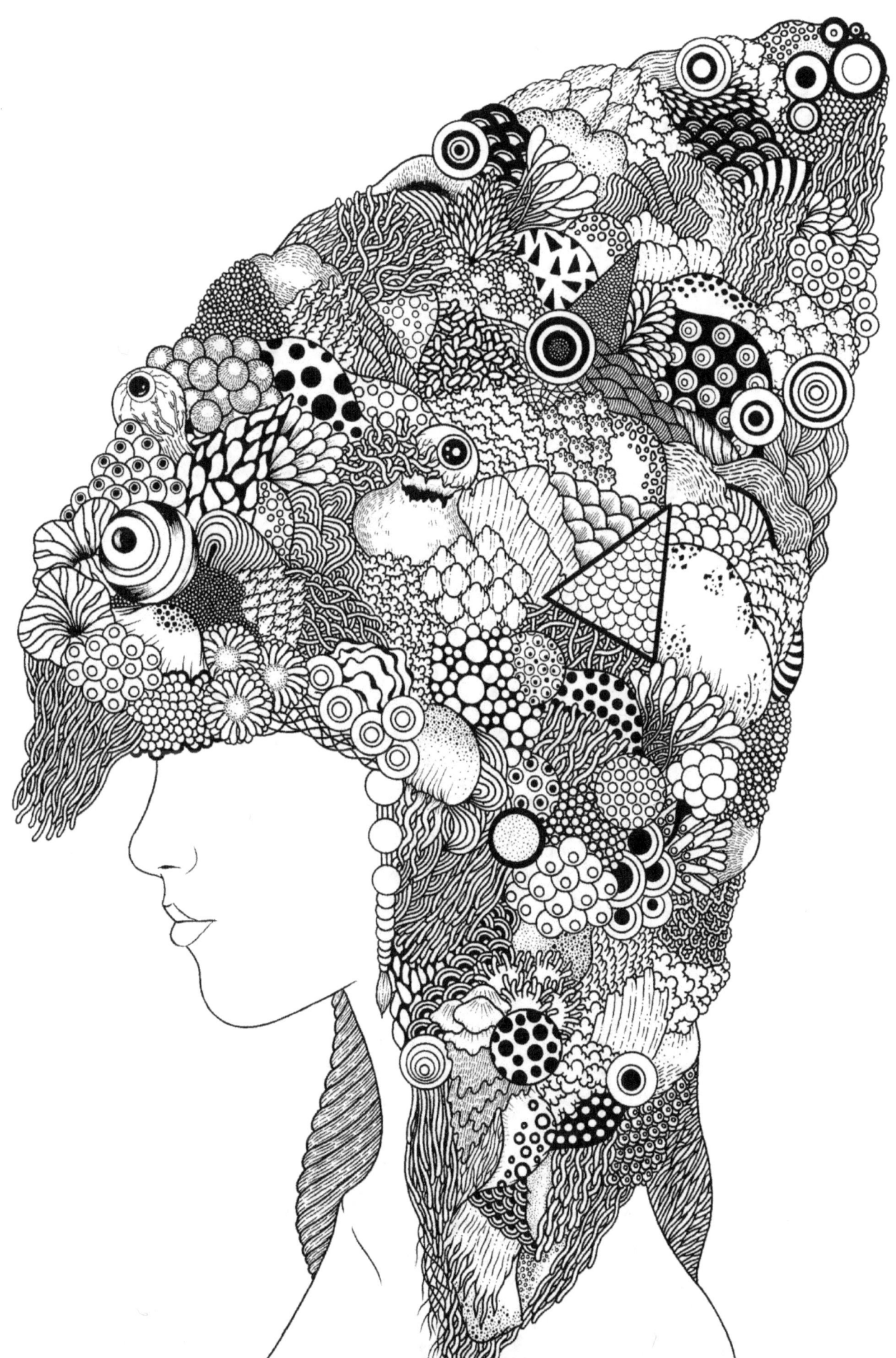

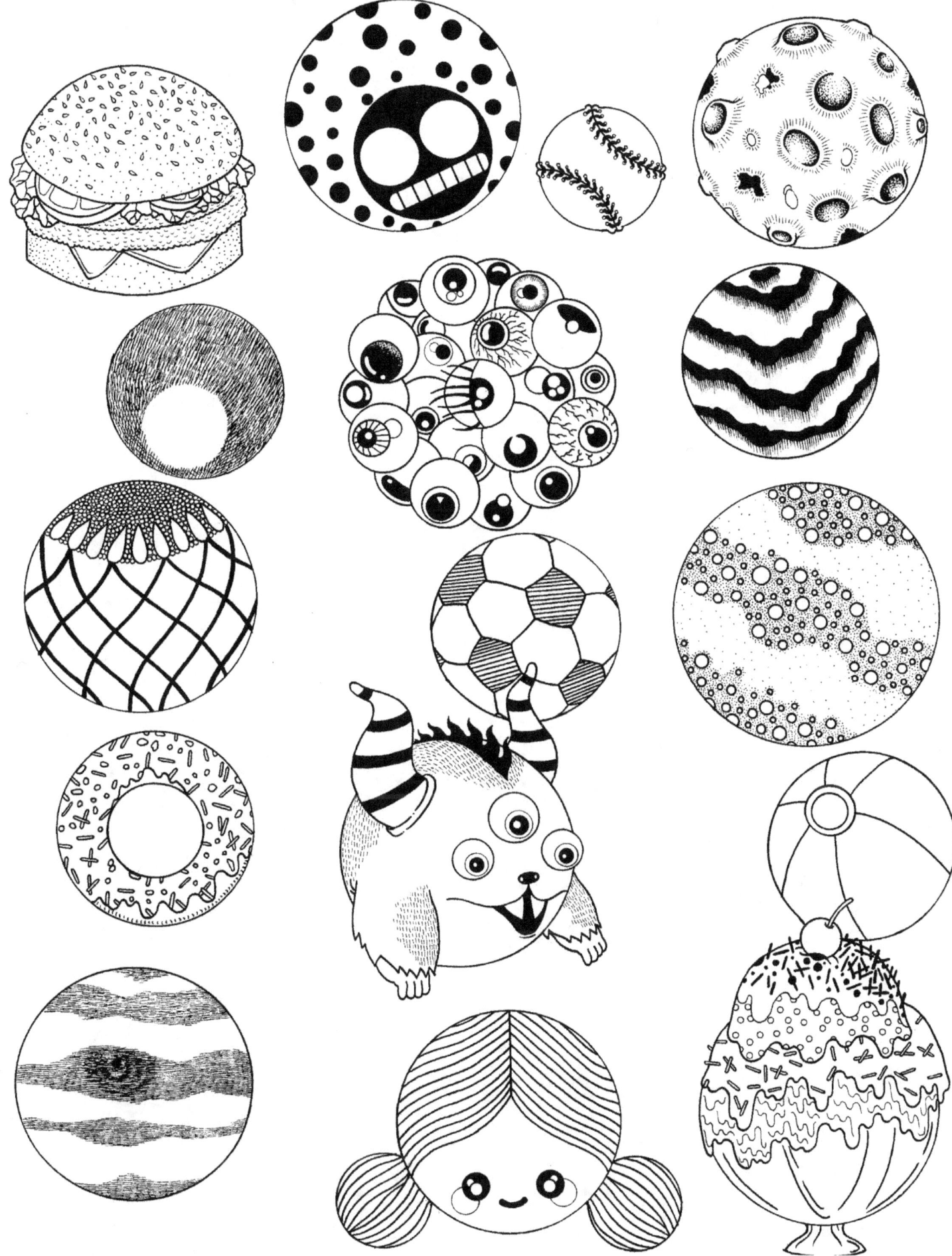

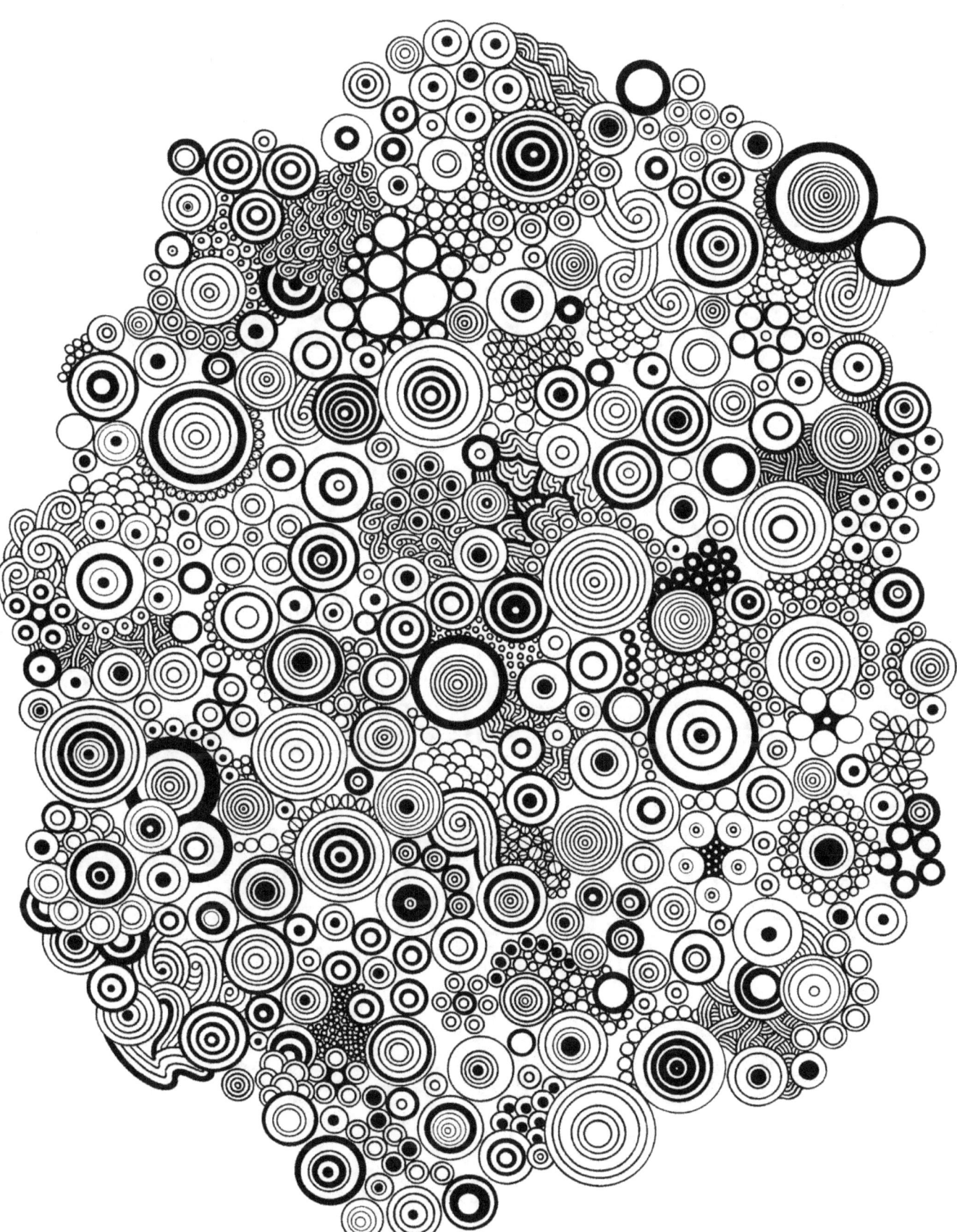

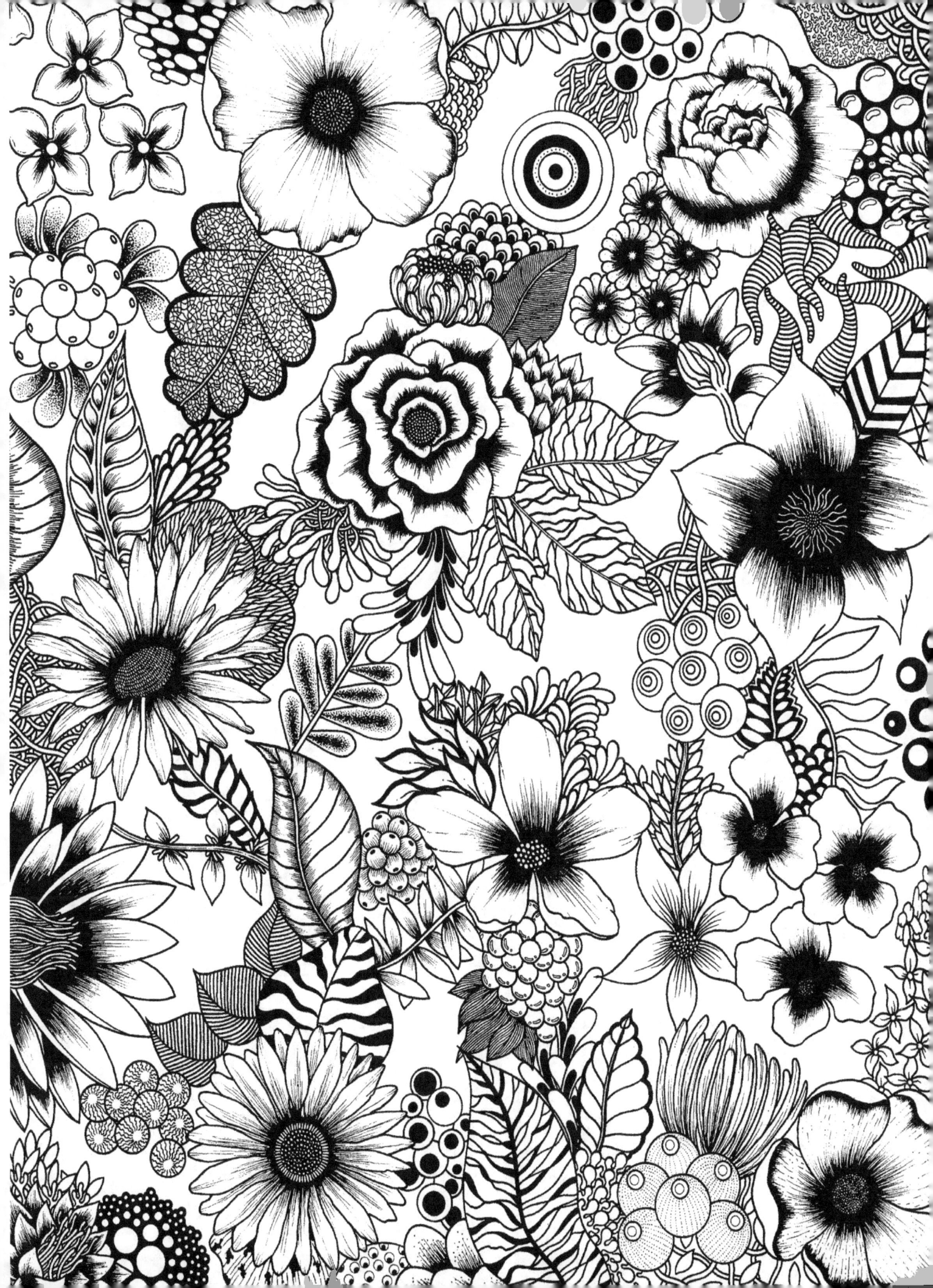

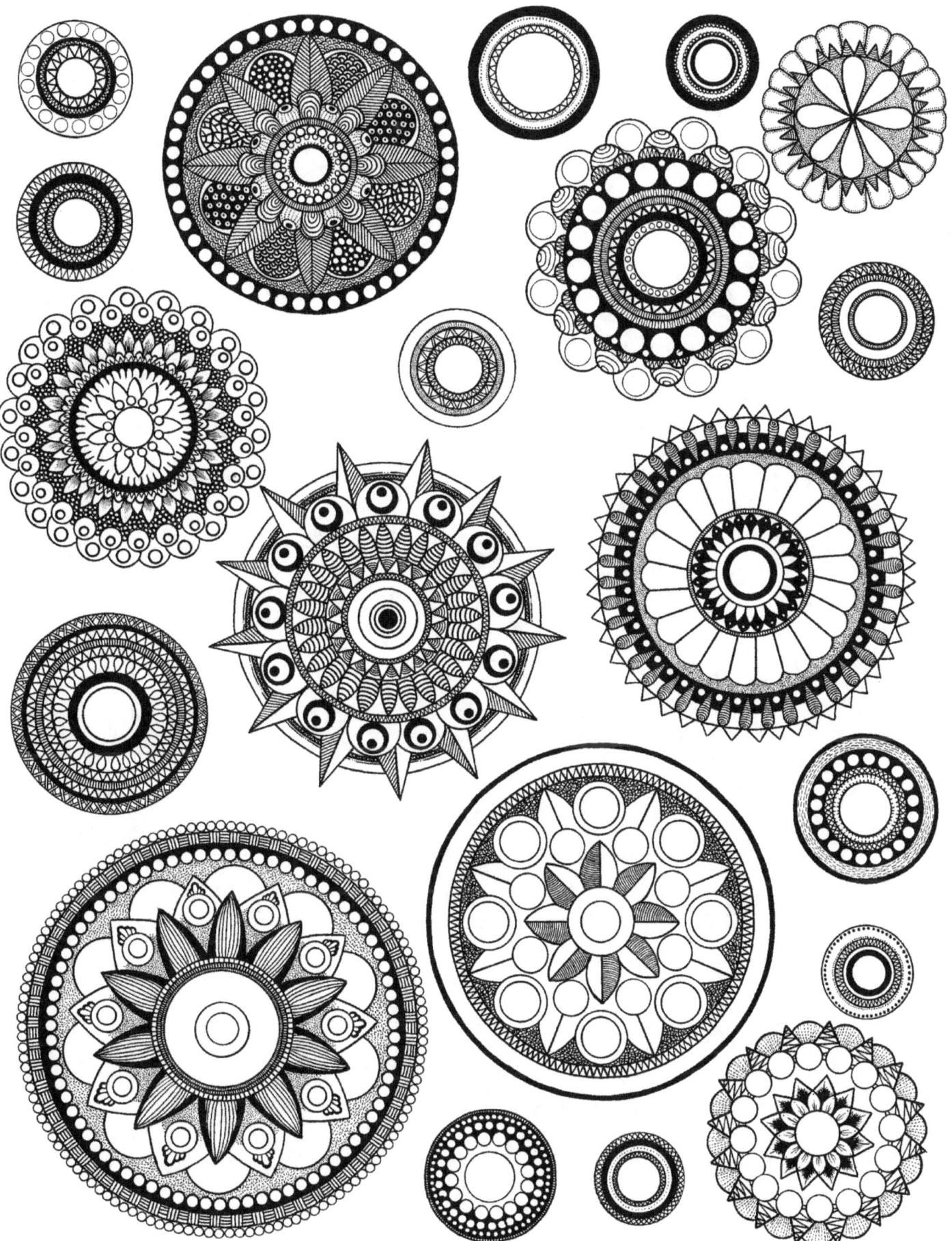

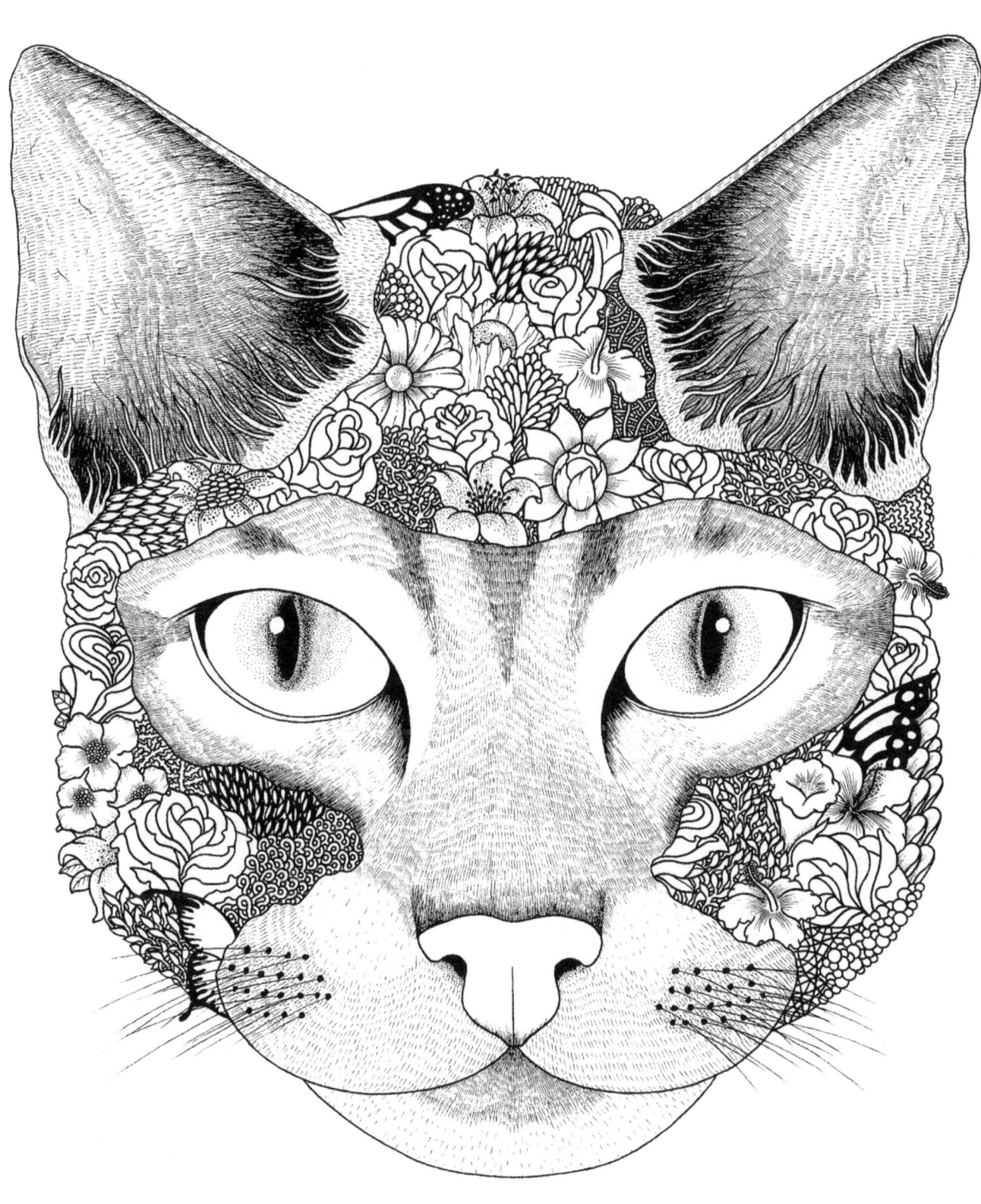

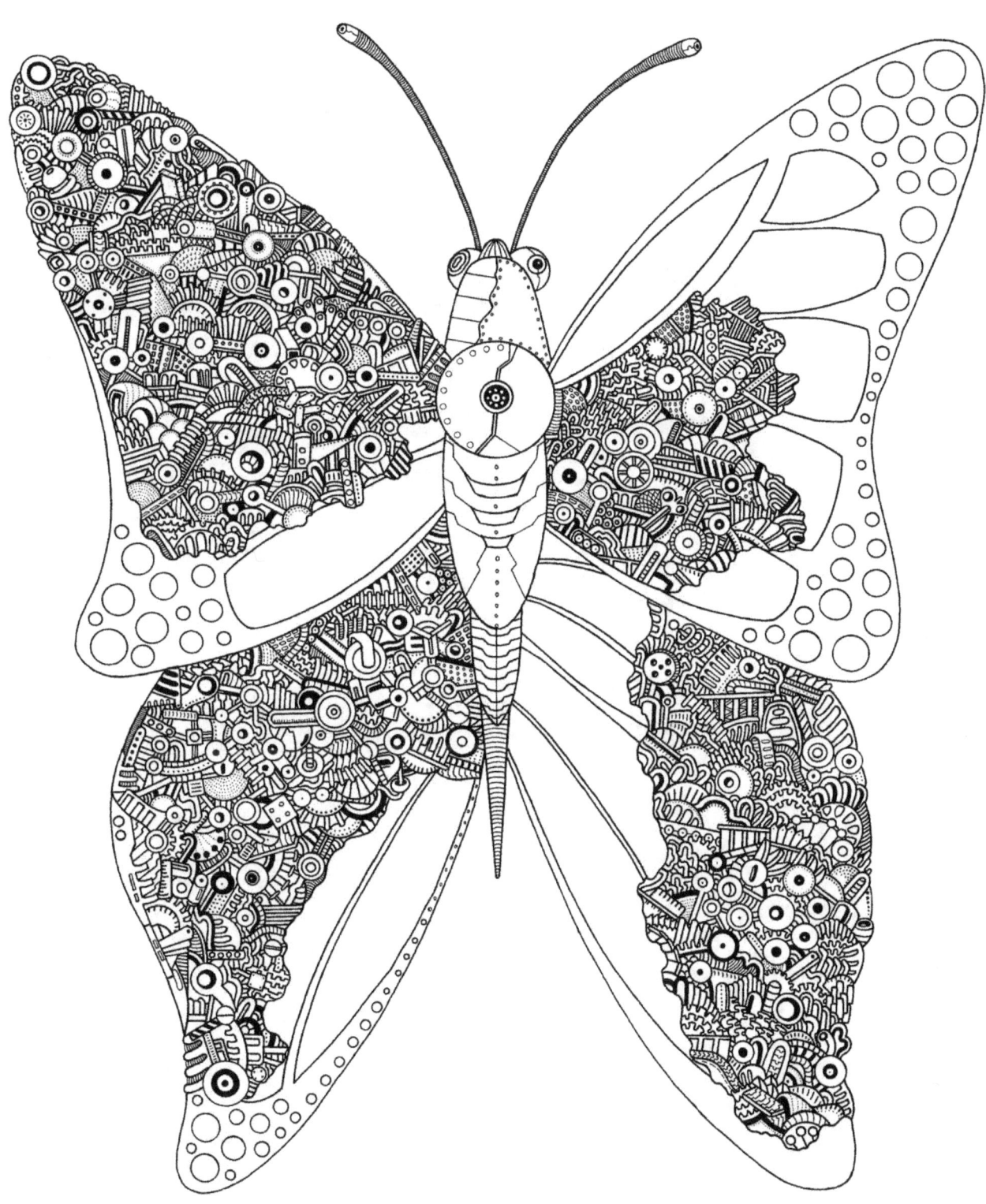

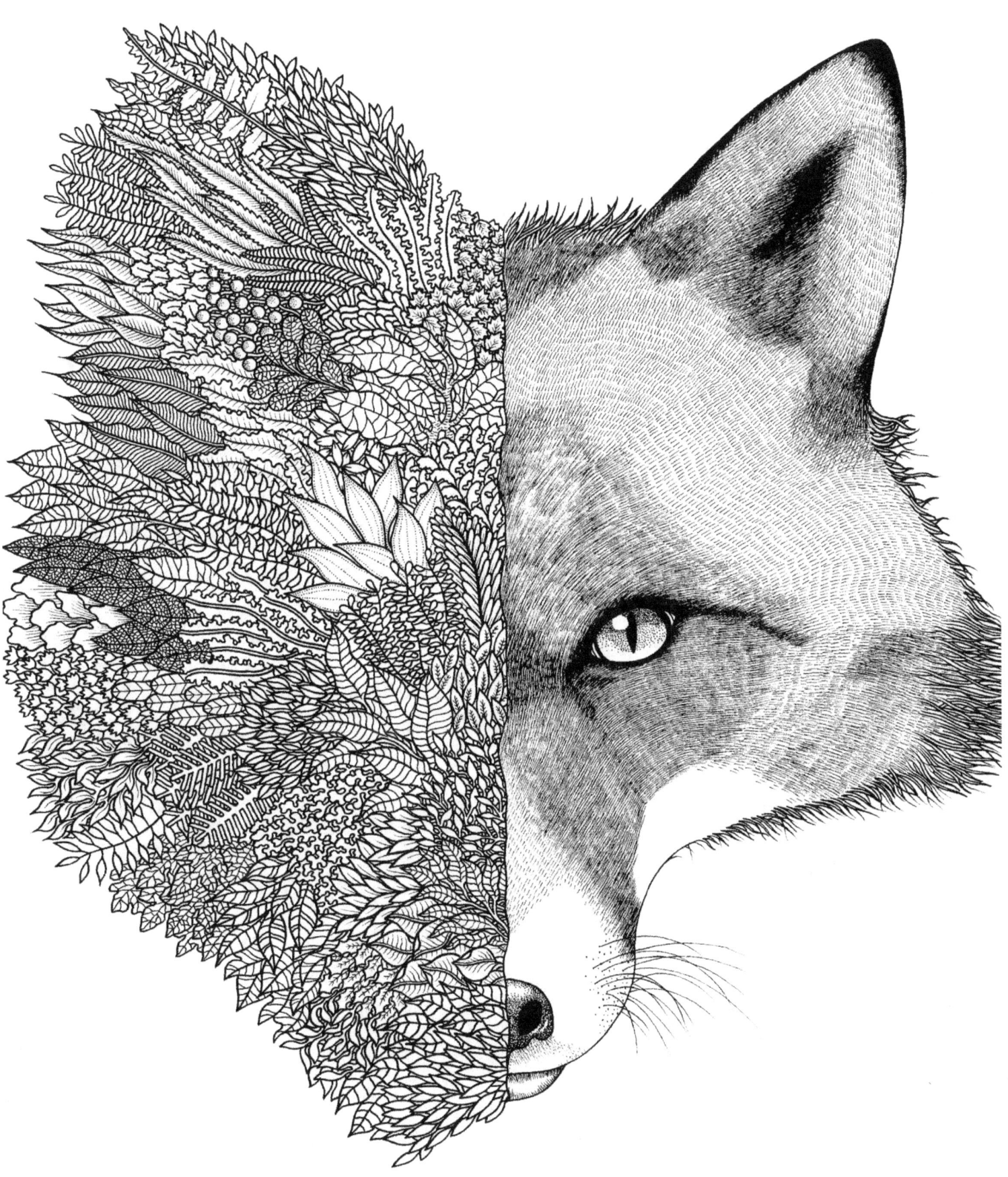

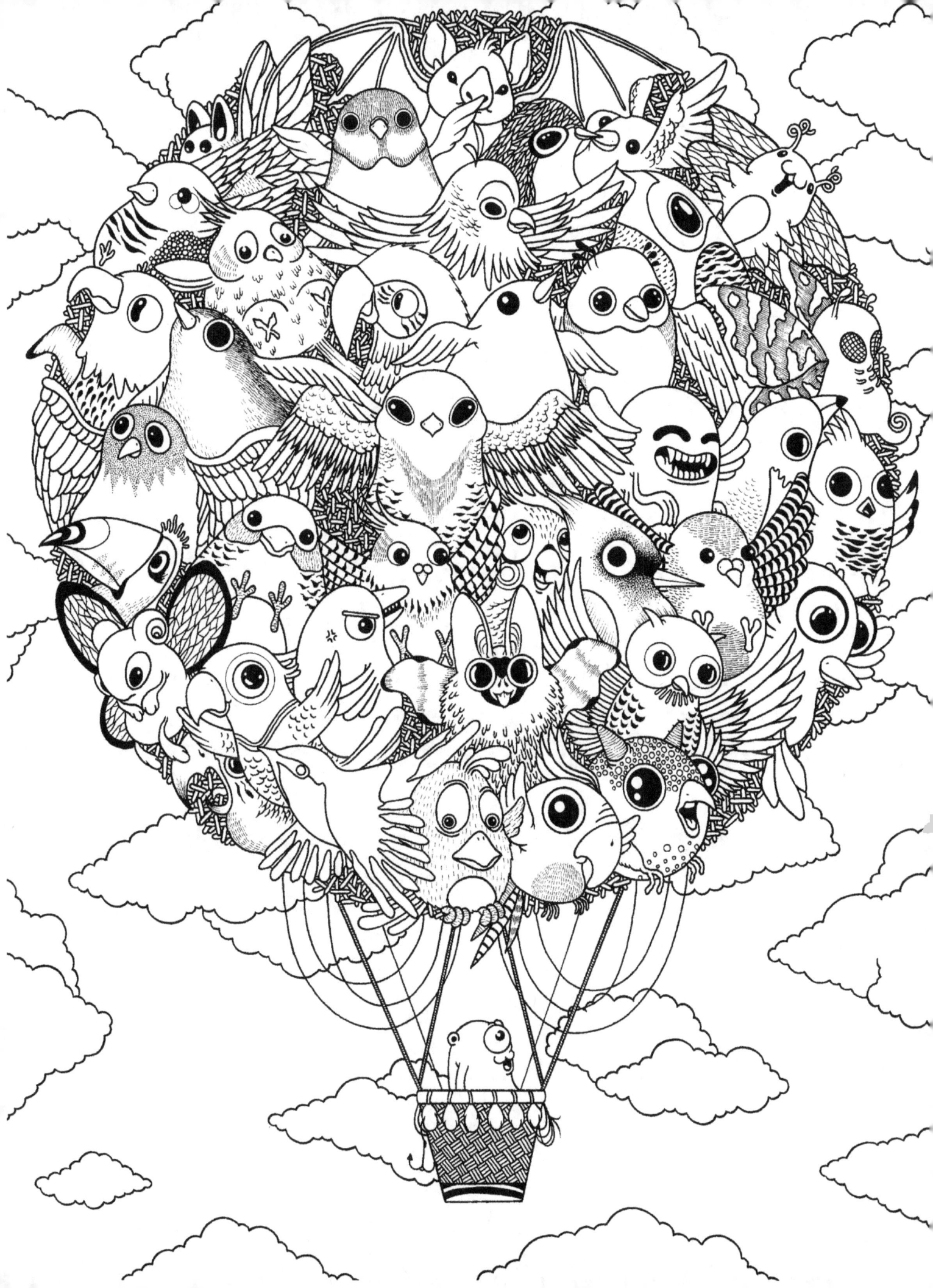

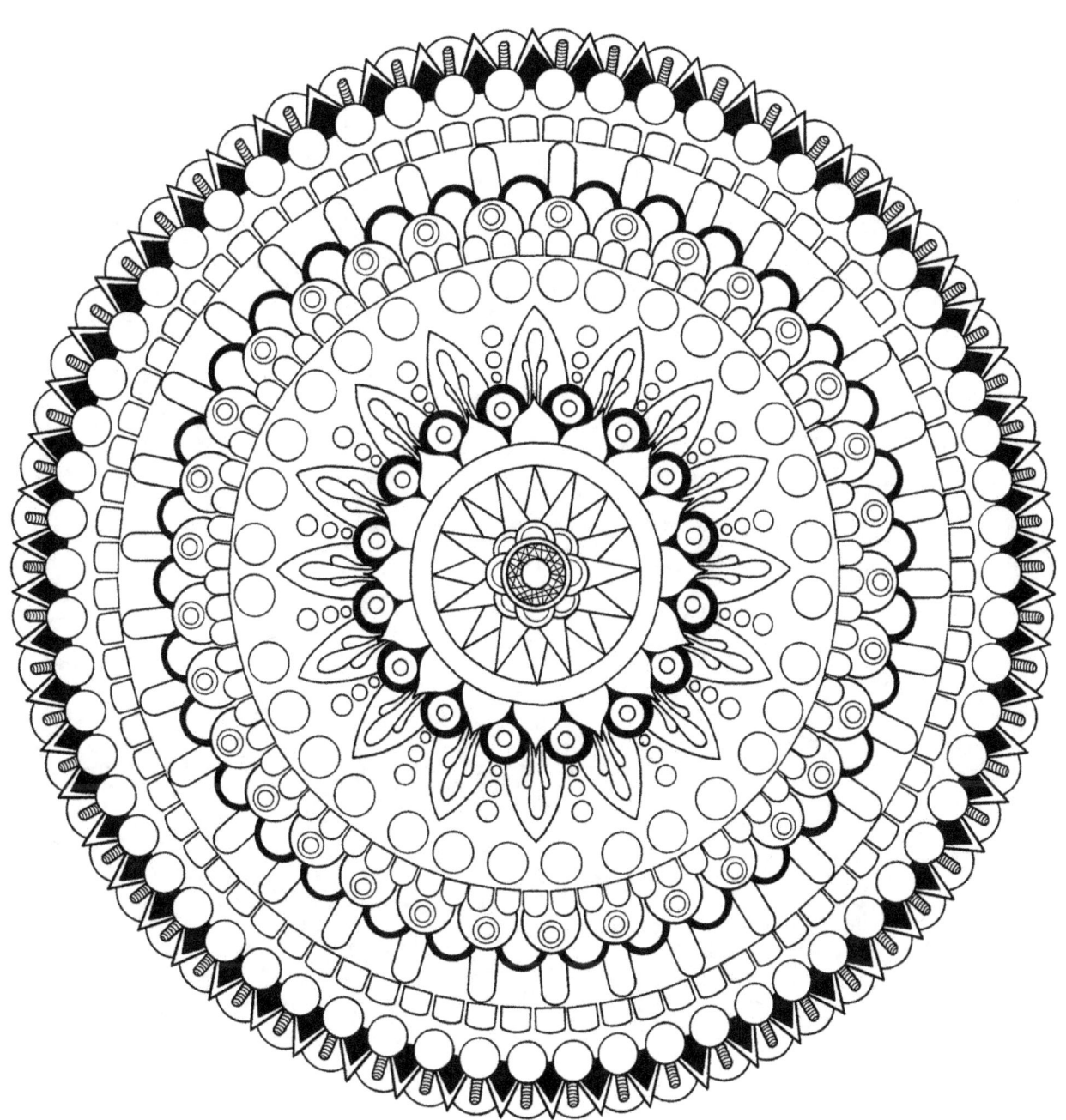

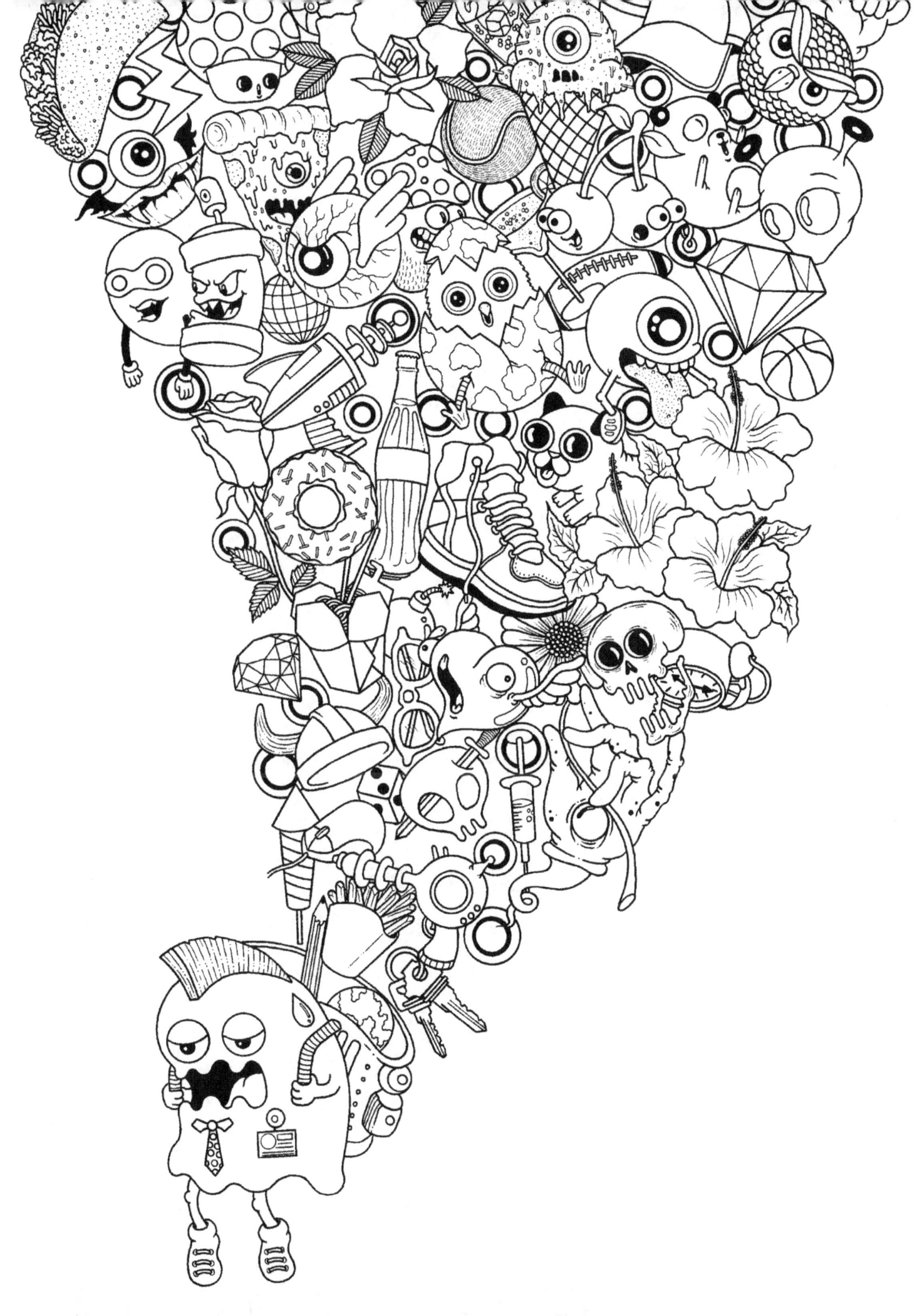

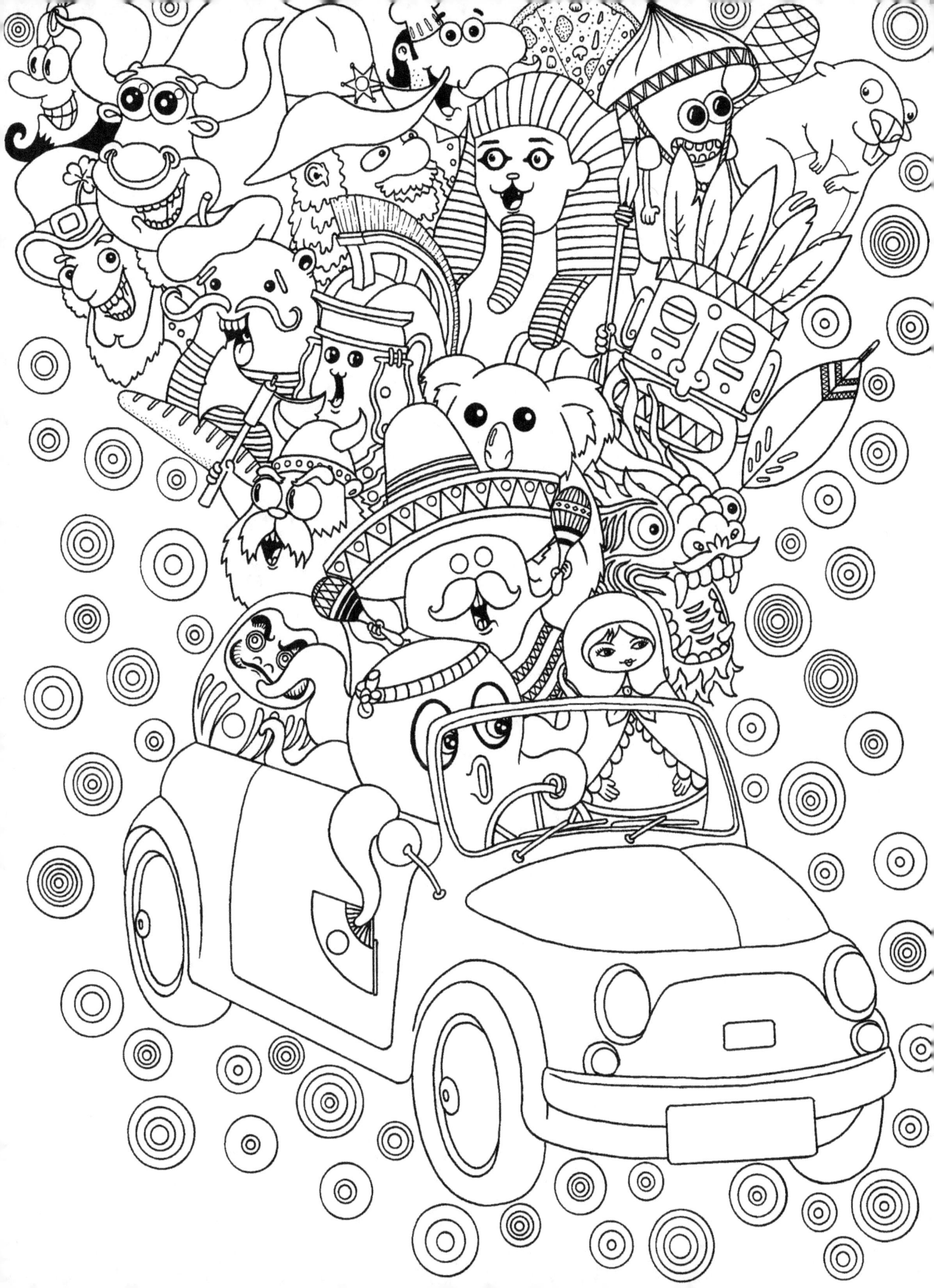

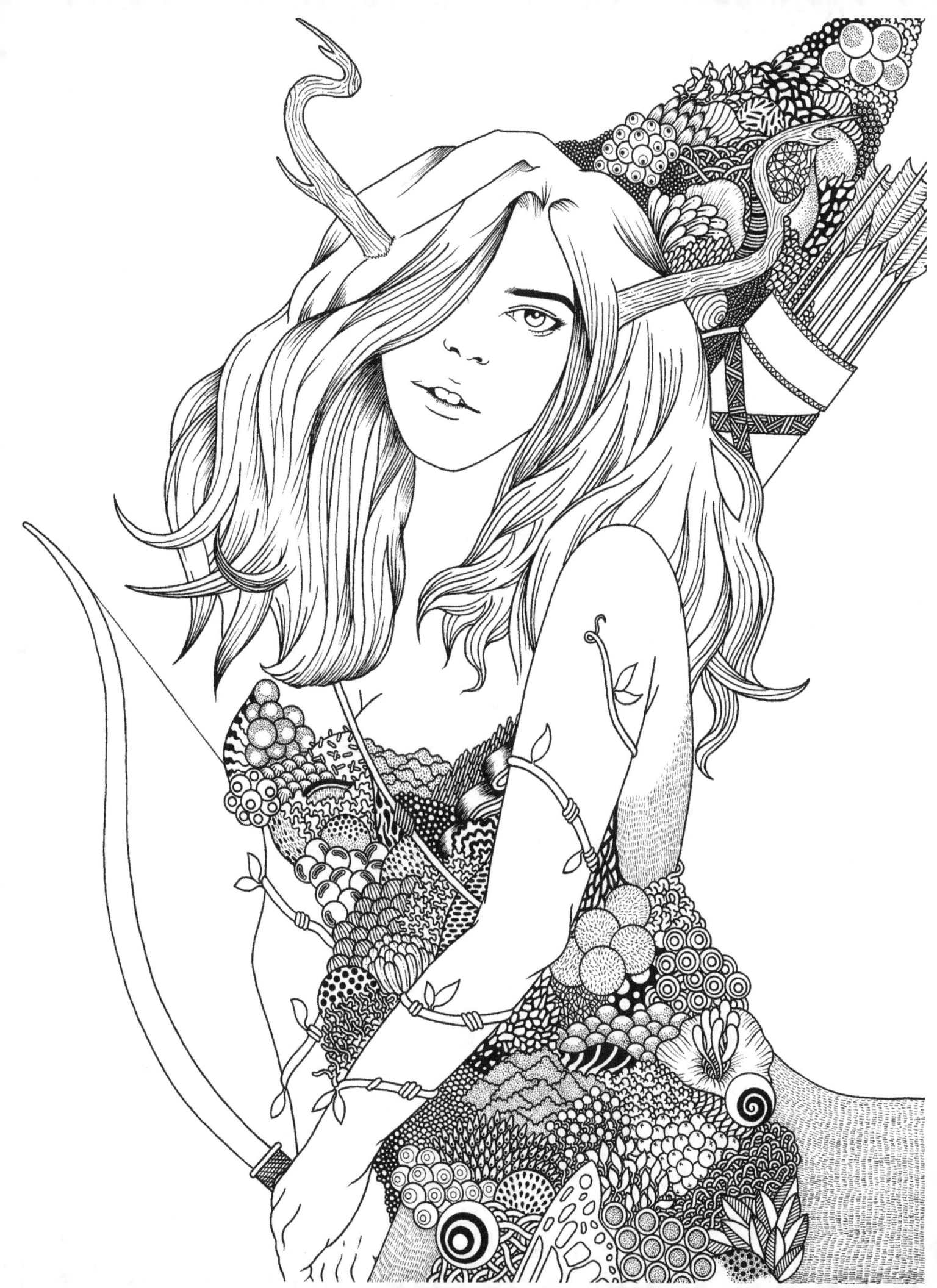

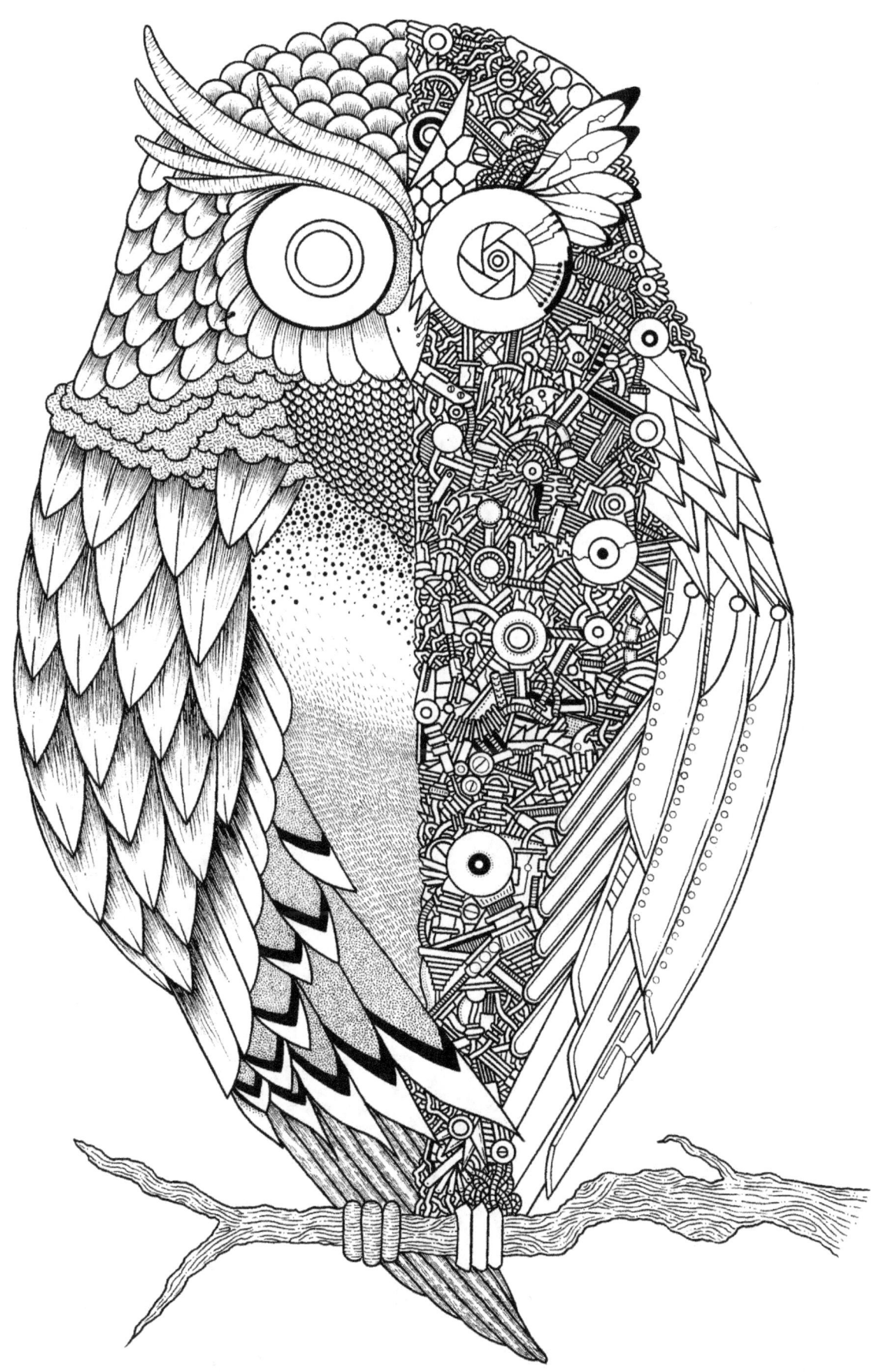

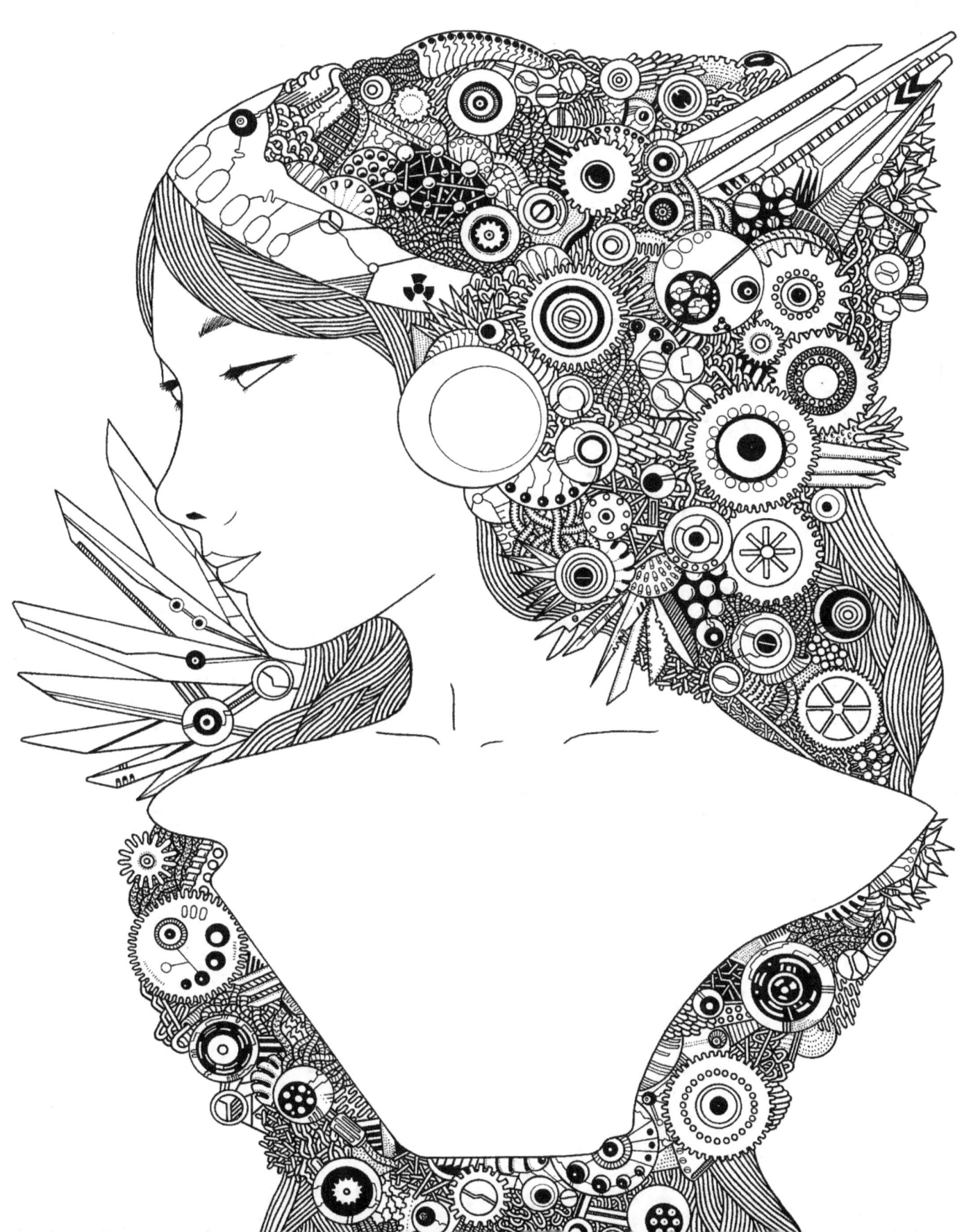

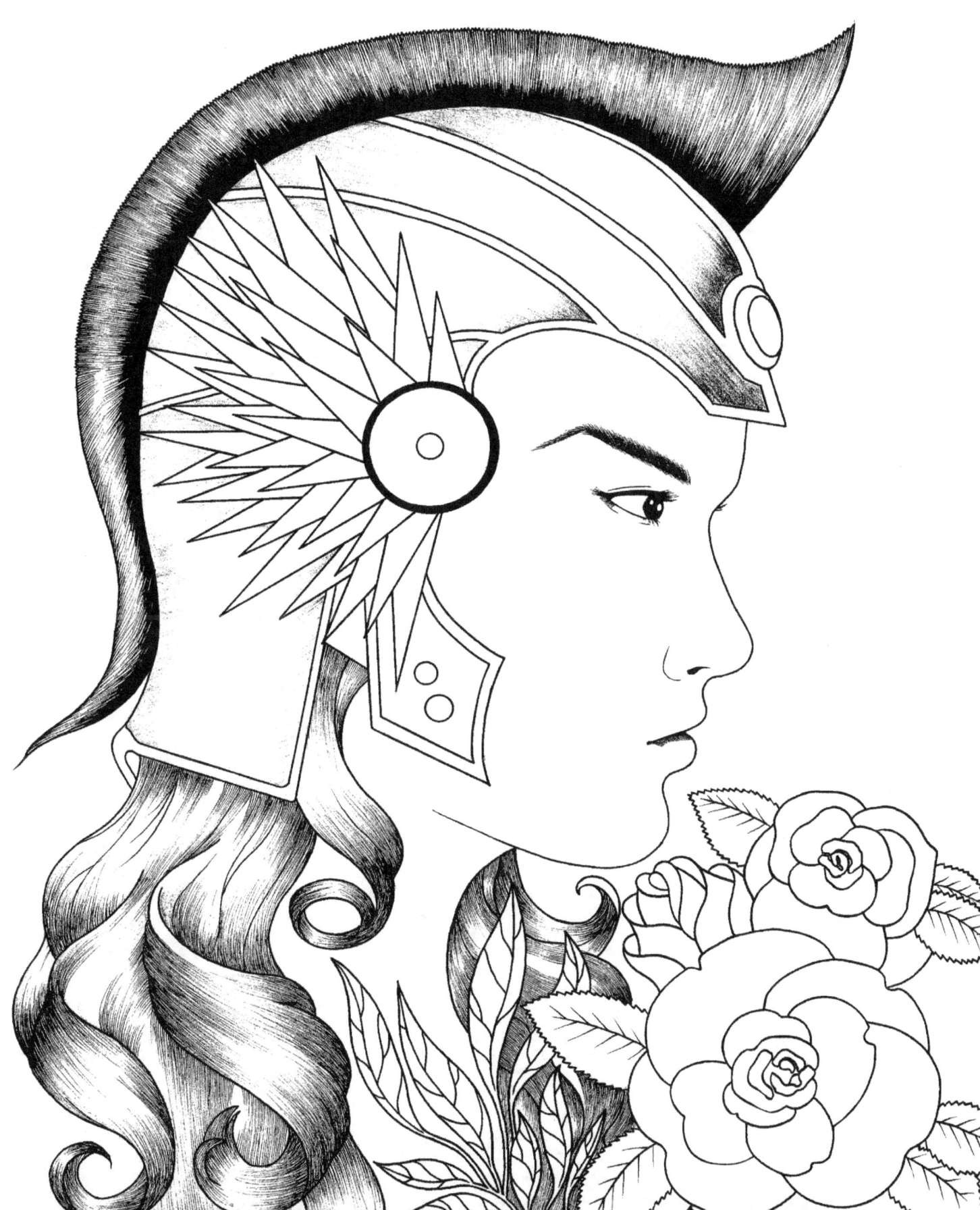

*Thank you
for buying this book,
your support means a lot
to me.*

Rocky Villaruel
www.rockyvillaruel.com
All rights reserved @2018

www.ingramcontent.com/pod-product-compliance
Lightning Source LLC
Chambersburg PA
CBHW062357220526
45472CB00008B/1835